Library of
Davidson College

THE NEW WORKER

Issued under the auspices of the
Shri Ram Centre for Industrial Relations

THE STUDY TEAM
DR. K. C. ALEXANDER

DR. S. D. KAPOOR

MR. S. P. BAJAJ

MR. K. N. VAID

The New Worker

A STUDY AT KOTA

K. N. VAID

ASIA PUBLISHING HOUSE
NEW YORK

© SHRI RAM CENTRE FOR INDUSTRIAL RELATIONS
NEW DELHI, 1968

PRINTED IN INDIA
BY MEGH RAJ AT THE NEW INDIA PRESS, CONNAUGHT CIRCUS, NEW DELHI
AND PUBLISHED BY P. S. JAYASINGHE ASIA PUBLISHING HOUSE,
29 EAST 10TH STREET, NEW YORK, N. Y. 10003

FOREWORD

INDIA is endeavouring to become a modern industrialized society. It is envisaged that industrialization would ensure a richer life for the people and provide a means that would transform the traditional society based on particularistic and ascriptive criteria to one based on universalistic and achievement standards. The country has made several strides in this direction. The process of change has touched new areas and brought into its fold people alien to an industrial culture. Who are the people that are drawn into this process? What is their social background? How significant is their socio-personal background in their adaptation to the new environment? What are their aspirations and expectations? How do they perceive their rewards, occupation, work situation, etc.? What are the effects of industrialism on their traditional values and standards? These are the questions with which those interested in industrialization—policy-makers, managers, administrators, and academicians—should be concerned. In his study of the new worker at Kota, Mr. Vaid undertakes to answer some of these questions.

It has been argued that the factory system is alien to, and in some respects incongruous with, the traditional Indian culture, and one could expect to find that people who are attracted to the new culture of industrialism are those who most feel the inadequacy of their traditional culture. This could happen either through the inability of persons to realize the values of the traditional society (landless people, for example), or through the failure of the traditional culture to meet a new set of aspirations and expectations.

We find that the new workers in Kota are subjected to all these forces. This does not, however, mean that the traditional background of persons has become totally irrelevant in the factory context. Certain elements of the traditional culture, such as caste status and the resultant educational achievement, influence one's status in the industrial society as well. Workers from higher castes find jobs in 'better' industries and those from lower castes gravitate towards 'lower' industries. This, in a way, indicates the limitation of industrialization itself to bring about fundamental changes in the social structure.

The success of the process of industrialization is in no small way dependent on the successful adjustment and adaptation of workers to the requirements of the factory system. Adjustment is dependent upon the expectations which the workers have about their occupation and their perception about the realization of those expectations. Wages, housing, job security, etc., are areas with which Kota workers were primarily concerned. On the other hand, their concern with things like work group and supervisory practices was insignificant. All this is relevant to the formulation of personnel policies aimed at the development of a well-adjusted industrial population. It also indicates the limited scope for introducing some of the advanced managerial concepts like participative management in the Indian set-up.

The study also explores in some depth the relationship between a worker's adjustment to work and his socio-personal background on the one hand and job situation on the other. On the personal side, education, job status, income, and migratory status were found to be positively related to adjustment. The level of technology used and the size and ownership of the plant were also found to facilitate the adjustment of workers. It is interesting to note that workers of a large privately owned plant were more adjusted than the workers of a publicly owned plant of similar size.

Mr. Vaid's study of the new workers at Kota, thus, makes a valuable contribution to our understanding of the emerging industrial workforce. Even though the study was confined to Kota, its findings should have relevance for other growth centres in the country. It is hoped that these findings are not only of academic interest, but would also be of some assistance to managers and policy-makers.

FOREWORD

This book is the second publication based on the study conducted by the Shri Ram Centre for Industrial Relations on the process of industrialization taking place at Kota. The study was made possible by a grant received from the Shriram Vinyl and Chemical Industries, Kota. I take this opportunity to thank the Company for their generous help.

ARUN JOSHI
Director

Shri Ram Centre for
Industrial Relations
New Delhi
May 1, 1968

PREFACE

THE credit for inspiring my interest in the study goes to Lala Charat Ram, Director of the Delhi Cloth & General Mills. By 1964, his PVC plant at Kota had gone into production. Two more giant enterprises to manufacture rayon cord and fertilizers were to follow. He was witnessing the stresses and strains that a new growth centre was undergoing along with those of the thousands of employees working for his companies. This aroused in him both curiosity and concern. At a chance meeting in early 1964, he mentioned the process of social change at Kota and suggested a visit to the area. The developments thereafter are reported on the following pages.

The credit for sustaining my interest in the study is due to Mr. Arun Joshi, Director of the Shri Ram Centre. He obtained a financial grant, developed result-centred supervisory practices and offered counsel at many a difficult moment. But for his patience and concrete support, the study might not have seen the printer's ink.

The field work, interviewing, and data collection for the study were done by Messrs Gurdial Singh, Krishen Verma, Harish Chhojar, and S. P. Bajaj. A camp office was set up at Kota under the charge of Mr. Bajaj. The field workers stayed at the project site for over six months and did commendable work under conditions of great physical discomfort. The initiative, tact, cheer, and academic rigour brought to bear by them on data collection and processing have been crucial to the success and quality of this project.

Mr. C. K. Basu, Department of Psychology, University of Delhi, helped in finalising the sample design. Prof. Fred C. Munson and Mr. Robert Gavin, both former Ford Founddation consultants at the Shri Ram Centre, gave constructive criticism of the study. My colleagues at the Centre Messrs B. M. Kapur, O. P. Dhingra, K. R. Seshagiri Rao, and D. K. Varma helped me at different stages of the study. And Mr. Stephen D'Costa typed the several drafts of the report. I am indebted to them for their generosity.

Finally, I express my gratefulness to the officers of the Department of Industries and Labour, Government of Rajasthan, all employers and contractors at Kota, and the 962 respondents for their cooperation in collecting data for the study. My research team and hundreds of respondents must share whatever credit the study might have. Yet, I alone am responsible for its shortcomings, for the conceptualisation, design, and write-up are mine.

New Delhi K. N. VAID
May 1, 1968

CONTENTS

FOREWORD	*v*
PREFACE	*ix*
LIST OF TABLES	*xiii*

I. HUMAN ADJUSTMENT TO FACTORY SYSTEM ... 1
    Conditions for Industrialization ... 1
    The Factory System ... 2
    Employee Adjustment to Work ... 5
    The Hypotheses ... 12
    The Significance of Kota ... 14
    The Study Design ... 14
    The Sampling ... 16
    The Data Collection ... 17
    The Chapter Scheme ... 20

II. KOTA AND ITS FACTORIES ... 21
    Introduction ... 21
    Demographic Changes ... 22
    The Nature of Industry ... 24

III. SOCIAL CHARACTERISTICS OF THE WORKFORCE ... 34
    Age ... 34
    Literacy and Level of Education ... 35
    Skill ... 36
    Background and Migration ... 37
    Caste ... 38
    Family Size and Composition ... 39
    Income ... 39
    Occupational Changes ... 41
    Income Changes ... 43
    Reasons for Job Changes ... 43
    Unemployment ... 44
    Social Selectivity ... 45
    Cultural Inadequacy ... 46
    Recruitment and Training ... 47
    Summary ... 49

IV. IN THE JOB MARKET ... 60
    Introduction ... 60

	Perception of Job Market	61
	Changes in Perceptions	62
	Entering the Job Market	65
	Education and Training	67
	Conclusions	69
V.	ADJUSTMENT TO WORK	76
	Introduction	76
	The Measure	76
	The Results	78
	Conclusions	89
VI.	THE IMAGE OF WORK	110
	Introduction	110
	The Results	111
	Conclusions	116
VII.	THE FINDINGS AND THEIR IMPLICATIONS	128
	The Findings	128
	The Implications	132
	APPENDICES	141
	INDEX	191

LIST OF TABLES

Table No.   *Page*

Chapter I

1. Table showing the universe, sample and the relative weightage given to each stratum — 18
2. Table showing the stratum-wise distribution of the respondents — 19

Chapter II

1. Table showing age distribution of respondents by job status — 50
2. Table showing age distribution of respondents by factory types — 50
3. Table showing age distribution of respondents by factory types and job status — 50
4. Table showing level of education of respondents by factory types — 51
5. Table showing level of education of respondents by factory types and job status — 51
6. Table showing classification of workers by skill in different factory types — 52
7. Table showing the background of respondents by factory types — 52
8. Table showing the place of origin of respondents by factory types — 52
9. Table showing caste distribution of respondents by job status — 53
10. Table showing caste distribution of respondents by factory types — 53
11. Table showing the family size of respondents by factory types and job status — 53
12. Table showing economic status of the members of respondents' families by factory types and job status — 54
13. Table showing monthly family income and per capita income of respondents by factory types — 54
14. Table showing distribution of workers by their 'take-home' pay and factory types — 55
15. Table showing distribution of workers by their gross salary and migratory status — 55
16. Table showing level of income and level of education of local workers — 55
17. Table showing respondents by number of previous employers by factory types — 56

18.	Table showing previous jobs held by respondents by occupation and by factory types	56
19.	Table showing respondents by occupation, previous jobs held and their fathers' occupations	56
20.	Table showing the location of previous jobs of respondents by factory types	57
21.	Table showing workers who held jobs previously by their highest monthly 'take-home' pay in any previous job	57
22.	Table showing respondents by their 'take-home' pay from the current job (CJ) and the highest ever 'take-home' pay from a previous job (PJ)	57
23.	Table showing the reasons for which respondents changed previous jobs	58
24.	Table showing distribution of respondents by duration of unemployment spells	58
25.	Table showing respondents according to each place of residence during unemployment by factory types	59
26.	Table showing respondents according to sources of livelihood during unemployment by factory types	59

Chapter IV

1.	Table showing distribution of respondents by length of service in their present employment	71
2.	Table showing respondents' length of service in the present employment by job status	71
3.	Table showing respondents' reasons for selecting the current job in the factory	72
4.	Table showing responses about respondents' search for future jobs if the current job is lost	72
5.	Table showing the distribution of respondents on 'what mattered most in getting a job'	72
6.	Table showing the distribution of respondents by the desired level of education by job status	73
7.	Table showing respondents by the purpose for which education is desired	74
8.	Table showing respondents by sources of vacancy information for the current job (CJ) and perceived sources for the future job (FJ)	74
9.	Table showing respondents by time taken to secure the current job and perception of time required to secure a job in the future	74
10.	Table showing respondents by time taken to secure the current job and the perception of time required to secure a job in the future by job status	75
11.	Table showing the distribution of respondents on 'the required basis for promotions'	75
12.	Table showing number of promotions earned by employees in their present employment by factory types	75

LIST OF TABLES

Chapter V

1. Table showing mean job attitude scores and standard deviations by factory types and job status of respondents — 79
2. Table showing the ranking of the means of twelve job status groups — 82
3. Table showing income and adjustment to work — 83
4. Table showing education and adjustment to work — 84
5. Table showing skill and adjustment to work — 85
6. Table showing age and adjustment to work — 86
7. Table showing origin and adjustment to work — 86
8. Table showing migration and adjustment to work — 87
9. Table showing caste and adjustment to work — 88
10. Table showing previous employment experience and adjustment to work — 88
11. Table showing dependency load and adjustment to work — 89
12. Table showing distribution of employees in the various age groups with their mean job satisfaction scores by types, by nature and by size of factories and by job status also — 92
13. Table showing distribution of employees in the various educational groups with their mean job satisfaction scores by types, by nature and by size of factories and by job status also — 94
14. Table showing distribution of employees in the skilled and unskilled groups with their mean job satisfaction scores by types, by nature and by size of factories and by job status also — 96
15. Table showing distribution of employees in the two groups according to their previous employment experience and their mean job satisfaction scores by types, by nature and by size of factories and by job status also — 98
16. Table showing distribution of employees in the various groups by their origin and their mean job satisfaction scores, by types, by nature and by size of factories and by job status also — 100
17. Table showing distribution of employees in the rural-urban groups with their mean job satisfaction scores, by types, by nature and by size of factories and by job status also — 102
18. Table showing distribution of employees in the various caste groups with their mean job satisfaction scores, by types, by nature and by size of factories and by job status also — 104
19. Table showing distribution of employees in the two groups according to dependency load, with their mean job satisfaction scores by types, by nature and by size of factories and by job status also — 106
20. Table showing distribution of employees in the various income groups with their mean job satisfaction scores, by types, by nature and by size of factories and by job status also — 108

LIST OF TABLES

Chapter VI

1. Table showing responses and relative rankings of employees' expectations in regard to certain job factors by types, by nature and by size of factories — 120
2. Table showing responses and relative rankings of employees' perceptions of certain job factors by types, by nature and by size of factories — 122
3. Table showing responses and relative rankings of employees' reactions to certain job factors by types, by nature and by size of factories — 124
4. Table showing discrepancy in employees' expectation, perception and reaction in ranking of certain job factors by nature, by size and by types of factories — 126

Appendix B

1. Table showing occupational time-rates of workers engaged through contractors in building and construction industry at Kota as fixed under the Minimum Wages Act, 1948 — 159
2. Table showing piece-rates for jobs done by workers employed through contractors in building and construction industry at Kota as fixed under the Minimum Wages Act, 1948 — 159
3. Table showing age distribution of respondents by job status — 163
4. Table showing literacy rate of respondents by job status — 164
5. Table showing levels of education of respondents by job status — 165
6. Table showing the origin of respondents by job status — 166
7. Table showing caste stratification of Hindu respondents by job status — 167
8. Table showing economic status of the members within a family — 168
9. Table showing family income, income per earner and per capita income of respondents by job status — 169
10. Table showing levels of income of respondents by job status — 169
11. Table showing in percentage the distribution of respondents according to the sources of vacancy information (for immigrants only) — 172
12. Table showing in percentage the distribution of respondents by age at the time of joining the first job — 173
13. Table showing in percentage the occupational mobility of respondents' two preceding generations — 174
14. Table showing in percentage the distribution of respondents according to the sources of vacancy information in respect of current and future jobs — 175
15. Table showing percentage distribution of respondents according to time taken to get the current job and expected time required to find a new job — 177

Chapter I

HUMAN ADJUSTMENT TO FACTORY SYSTEM

Conditions for Industrialization

CURRENTLY, about two-thirds of mankind is undergoing a great economic and social transformation. The developing nations are eager to achieve mastery over science and technology to ensure for themselves a richer and more satisfactory life. Contemporary Western society is a constant reference category, at least insofar as its material prosperity is concerned. Some nations may adopt science and technology to suit their cultural conditions, social patterns, and value-orientation; others may adapt themselves to the former. Whatever be the model of social adaptation to technology, the logic of industrialization dictates that a nation must strive to make greater use of inanimate sources such as power, and of tools that multiply the effect of effort.

The experience of developed countries also shows that, although the process of industrialization is by no means unilineal, some of its requirements are inflexible. At the societal level, a developing country must acquire cohesive bonds of nationhood, a strong and stable government and a broad national consensus on basic economic, social, and political objectives. Further, it requires a legal and administrative framework that permits economic institutions and organizations to function, provides incentives for entrepreneurship and opportunities for capital formation. The 'achievement' standards should replace 'ascription' standards as the basis of social gradation, and universalistic considerations be accepted as the normative basis for role relationship. At the individual level, people should have faith in both the desirability and the possibility of the change. They should have a desire for higher achievement and better living standards, favourable attitudes towards work, risk-taking, mobility, and empathy, possess ability to put off immediate satisfactions for higher gains in the future and certain norms of social, economic, and political discipline that are necessary for the achievement of the national objectives. Thus, social adaptations and human adjustments that are concomitant to technological changes remain the major influences on economic development.

The Factory System

The factory system (in contradistinction to the guild or domestic system) of production ideally meets the above-stated criteria that are necessary for the process of industrialization. Through the application of rational techniques of production, such as budgeting, accounting, and rules of operation, it offers wide opportunities for increases in efficiency and productivity. As a result, the search of the developing nations for a new future and a new identity has become synonymous with their aspirations and struggles in establishing extensive factory systems.

The factory system permits a pattern of economic activity in which the methods of production of goods and services can be rationally used. Power drawn from inanimate sources and all kinds of machines and tools are used to multiply the effect of the efforts of operatives who work under one roof. The operatives' role in the production process is determined by those who select the technology (the employer, the managers), the level of technology used, and the work group. The factory system may, thus, be viewed as a system of role relationship between the worker and the employer/managers on the one hand, and the technology and the work group in the context of the work situation on the other. This argument deserves further examination.

A factory system establishes two economic groups, *viz.*, the employer/managers and the workers. The former have the right to take decisions on economic and technological matters and to direct the efforts of others. The latter have the responsibility of following the directions in return for the gains they receive. The rights and responsibilities of both parties are laid down through a set of rules pertaining to recruitment, work standards, wages, working conditions, hours of work, job security, discipline, grievances, fringe benefits, etc. Theoretically, the labour market pulls govern the nature of these rules; but in practice, they are very complicated. The political system of the country, the economic conditions of the industry, the availability of the required skills, the unionization of workers, the philosophy of the management, etc., are some of the constraints on purely labour-market-based work rules. Again, as the motives and interests of the parties differ, periodic clashes (strikes, lock-outs, go-slows, etc.) are unavoidable. Thus, the factory system creates two economic groups (management and workers), pyramids of hierarchies within the enterprise (managers, foremen, supervisors, etc.), and an elaborate network of rules that establish the relationships among these different hierarchies. Whereas the opposing economic interests of the parties might lead to a breakdown of the enterprise, the work rules tend to keep it going. The adjustment between the two forces is a continuous process and calls for new patterns of rule-making. There is full and rapid acceptance of rules if both the parties (the traditional rule-makers and those who are affected by the rules) have a hand in making them. The factory system is, thus, not only rational but democratic as well.

The influence of technology on social relations in the work situation is significant. The level of technology, flow of work, speed of machines, etc., are often the decisive factors in ordering the required skills, in determining the occupational status of workers, and in arranging the social relations at work. An automated or semi-automated production process uses superior technology and requires a relatively small number of high-skilled operatives. A precision tool-making plant uses technology which calls for operatives skilled enough to control and operate machines and direct their output. There the quality of the product is linked to the skill of the operative. On the other hand, only such workers who can perform repetitive operations are required in an assembly-line process. Here individual operatives are grouped by the type of machines they tend or the nature of the product of the machines. The operations require minimal skills which soon reach their peak and then taper off. Similarly, industries that are engaged in processing raw material or civic services (gas, water, electricity) require gang labour. Skills are required only at the supervisory level.

Technology not only orders skills in the plant, it has an influence on the size of work group, the status stratification on the shopfloor, and the role relationship among men in the different strata as well. This influence is of a basic nature. The size of the work group, in turn, conditions the degree of formalization of work rules. The ordering of skills affects the wage structure as well as the wage bill of the plant. Occupational stratification has implications for reporting relationships and supervisory patterns.

Specialization of work is another aspect of the factory system. Division of labour results in work simplification and its standardization, reduction in training costs, and low skill requirements at each point of production. It also demands less of workers' energy. All this gives continuity to the production process, and helps to increase output and reduce costs. Further, it defines the specific roles which individual workers can play in the factory, and the manner in which those roles are to be related. It also tends to establish the status of the worker on the basis of his skill, work, and wages. Division of labour, however, induces certain strains on the workforce. Work standardization and routine and repetitive work reduce the need for skill in production and make the worker an appendage of the machine. All this affects him psychologically. Monotony, boredom, lack of interest in work, and a feeling of insecurity in the job are the inevitable consequences.

Economically dependent as he is upon the enterprise, the operative becomes a part of its hierarchical structure, wherein he stands at a low level. The technology determines his status, defines his role, and orders his relationship with the others in the hierarchy. What is expected of him, and what he can expect from others and the plant, are specified in the work rules. Sometimes, he also has a hand in the formulation of work rules. The division of work leads to his performance of work of a very circumscribed character which perhaps consumes less of his energy, but demands more of physical and psychological adjustment to work rhythms.

The tenets of the factory system, of which the worker is a part, are different from those of the traditional social system in which the worker is born. The kinship ties that gave the worker access to economic pursuits in the traditional society are superseded by education, training, and skill in the factory system. The worker's earnings and standard of living are no longer attributions of the economic position of his family. They are, by and large, determined by his own output in the new order. Caste and family, which constitute the basis of social gradation in the traditional society, are replaced by occupational designation, nature of work done, and wages earned in the new set-up. The pressures of existence and the need to thrive in the new system compel the worker to revise his concept of family responsibility and his attitude towards superiors. Fixed earnings and shortage of housing often lead him to make a choice between the nuclear family and the joint family. The desire to improve his working conditions motivates him to seek a voice in rule-making processes in the plant. These tenets of the factory system make the worker realize that it may be profitable to him if he joins hands with similarly situated workers—not necessarily kinship or caste groups—and raise demands. The polarization of positions in the traditional society and the factory system may not exist at present, but the trends in that direction are fairly obvious.

We may conclude that the factory not only introduces new methods of production but also initiates changes in the forms of social structure, value-orientation, motivation and norms of people. Therefore, modern technology cannot be sustained and made fully productive without bringing fundamental changes in the dimensions of personality, culture, and society.

Employee Adjustment to Work

The Concept

Under the impact of the factory system, a society undergoes transformation at the technological, structural, and behavioural levels. The efficiency and productivity of the system depend upon the degree of consonance among the changes at all the three levels. The forms of changes at the technological and structural levels have been discussed in the preceding section. We shall now turn to the changes at the behavioural level.

The new modes of production and the associated forms of social structure require individual workers to make new adjustments. They are continuously called upon to achieve a harmonious mental and behavioural balance between their own personal needs and strivings, and the demands of others both in the work situation and in the social environment. Thus, human adjustment to the factory system is a process of continuous interaction between the personal goals and behaviour of individual worker, and the demands of technology, management, work rules, and the work group. In the process of adjustment to work, an employee, consciously or unconsciously, modifies his own behaviour and norms of output, pace, and purpose to suit the requirements of the work.

Adjustment could be regarded as an achievement, which may be good or bad. This practical way of looking at adjustment has several advantages. First, it permits comparisons of the workers in terms of their capacity for adjustment. Second, it helps in distinguishing job satisfaction from adjustment to work at the conceptual level. A person with low expectations can acquire job satisfaction which may not mean adjustment with a system in which 'achievement' is the norm. Third, it enables enterprises to foster consciously work rules that generate incentives for functional alterations in human behaviour and give direction to the process of interaction.

Characteristics of an Adjusted Employee

A few dimensions of the human personality may be mentioned to show the characteristics of an employee with a higher adjustment to work. Greater empathy (capacity to perceive work as perceived by others in the organization), mobility (ability to switch from one status to another or from one set of roles to another), and high participation (active participation in a variety of divergent roles in a wider arena arising out of a release from, or low priority assigned to, the traditionally constricted sphere of activity) in an individual show his superior adjustment. The ability to make a rational ends-means calculation is another characteristic of this type. An adjusted person is also noted for his sense of independence and self-sufficiency which enable him to depend on his own judgement in personal goal-setting and actions, and to display initiative and creativity. A sense of responsibility is also required for a satisfactory adjustment. The adjusted person takes into account the consequences of his actions and considers the long-range effects of his behaviour. He must also find his self-concept acceptable, accept others, and display a sense of time perspective. He does not plot out the present by re-living the past or by dreaming about the future. Finally, a well adjusted person has a problem-solving attitude. He is willing to face problems, tries to understand them, and works out solutions.

Factors that Influence Adjustment

Several factors influence employee adjustment to work. They can be identified under three categories, *viz.*, institutional, job, and socio-personal.

(A) INSTITUTIONAL FACTORS

The institutional factors refer to various aspects of the enterprise in which an employee works. The level of technology used, the ownership of the plant, the size of the factory in terms of employment, and the job status assigned to an employee constitute the most important factors in this category. It is our hypothesis that superior technology, private ownership, bigger size of the plant, and higher job status of an employee make for a higher employee adjustment to work.

Technology: Superior technology offers several stimuli that make for a higher adjustment. First, handling of complicated machines and complex production processes is, in itself, a source of greater satisfaction to the operatives. Making a monstrous machine respond to a twist of the finger, or controlling the flow of tonnes of material by pressing a knob, gives a feeling of elation to the operatives. Second, superior technology requires men with higher skills, gives recognition to workers' education and training, provides them with higher remuneration, and enables them to move up in the organization and occupy key and supervisory positions. Thus, by enhancing the operatives' shopfloor status and by giving them recognition, technology exercises a pull towards higher adjustment. Third, superior technology contributes to the operatives' prestige in the work community. Fourth, superior technology is rarely labour intensive. It tends to keep the work group small and thus affords more opportunities for satisfactory social relations at the work place. Finally, it offers the operatives a feeling of security that comes from their indispensability to the organization, their possession of quickly salable skills, and from working more closely with senior personnel. Thus, persons working in an automated plant or those engaged in machine control operations could be expected to be better adjusted as compared to those who work in assembly and processing factories. The latter should, in turn, show superior adjustment when compared with those working in utilities and services.

Ownership: Ownership of the enterprise is another institutional factor that affects employee adjustment to work. Basically, the issue revolves round the 'private *versus* public' ownership of enterprises. The private enterprises that exist for making profits are primarily efficiency-oriented, even though many of them may not be working at the desired level of efficiency. By definition, they are more flexible in accommodating, promoting, compensating, and rewarding talent of the desired type. They are expected to pay better, base promotions on demonstrated ability, share profits in the form of bonus, etc. They are quick to recognize initiative, creativity, risk-taking qualities in their personnel and offer rewards for the same. Thus, the value-orientation and the basis of employee gradations in private enterprises are in conformity with the logic of industrialism. Public enterprises show a degree of difference on all these counts. They, too, value efficiency, but the civil service rules which are the source of plant level policies impose severe restraints on its achievement. This limits their ability to respond to local considerations in matters of recruitment, wage structure, etc., and exposes them to the pressures of social justice as implied in the political system of the country. The bureaucratic procedures cause delays in recognizing and rewarding innovation and initiative, with the result that the incentive value is lost in the process. The employees suffer from the conflict created by the demands of efficiency and the lack of opportunities afforded by the public enterprises to meet them. In view of these arguments, we hypothesize that employees working in private enterprises will be better adjusted to work as compared to those working in public undertakings.

Size: The size of the plant has a relevance to employee adjustment. Big plants have, of necessity, to develop structural hierarchies and elaborate work rules to link them. The rights and duties of individuals and groups must be stated in unambiguous terms. Procedures need to be developed whereby an individual can relate his role with others, or can seek redress if he fails to do so. Large plants have invariably a better record of compliance with labour laws and are likely to have a stronger union force. Efficient communication systems, well-defined rights and responsibilities, greater promotion opportunities, the strength of numbers, more and better statutory benefits—all attributes of larger size—tend to contribute to superior employee adjustment to work.

Job Status: It is also hypothesized that the higher the job status of an employee in an organization, the higher will be his adjustment to work. The hypothesis is based on the assumption that a higher job status motivates an employee to identify himself more closely with the organization. The harmony—that is a reduction of conflict—between personal goals and organizational goals leads to higher adjustment to work. Further, higher job status also means more recognition, status, prestige and, very often, more money. All these factors contribute to superior adjustment to work. We do not contend that clerks have a better job status than that of workers, but supervisors certainly possess a higher job status than that of the other two groups. We should expect to find that supervisors are better adjusted than clerks or workers, irrespective of the level of technology and the nature of the enterprise.

(B) JOB FACTORS

The job consists of several intrinsic factors, such as wages, employment security, hours and conditions of work, opportunity for advancement, supervision, workload, physical environment, work group, fringe benefits, etc. An employee's reaction to the job and its intrinsic factors conditions his desire to modify his behaviour so as to achieve harmony with the demands of work and, thereby, to adjust to it. If an employee expects high wage and fringe benefits from his job, and perceives it to be providing both, his reaction to it can be expected to be favourable, leading to higher adjustment. On the other hand, if he looks for quick promotions but perceives that the job does not permit them, he is likely to react unfavourably and be less adjusted to it.

Employees' expectations from their jobs and their perceptions thereof are influenced by several economic and social factors. Earnings may continue to fall short of pecuniary needs in an inflationary economy. The family grows faster than the pay packet for most employees, particularly the young. The improvement in the economic status of a person, generally, generates more demands on him by the members of the extended family and relatives, with the result that the money available per capita may not improve. Job security may assume primary importance in conditions where unemployment is rife. Housing, schooling, and other community services may be desired, particularly by immigrants to new growth centres. The patterns of individual expectations from the job and of the conditions that create such expectations may vary, but the employees' reaction to the job factors and the resultant adjustment will invariably be the function either of discrepancy or of consistency between the expectation and the perception on one or more job factors.

(C) SOCIO-PERSONAL FACTORS

The social quality of the workforce may be related to its adjustment to work. It can be expected that superior social quality will make for a better adjustment to work. Young age apart, higher levels of education and skill, upper caste, higher income level, urban origin, longer employment standing, less unemployment in work experience, and greater mobility are generally taken as indicators of the superior social quality of a workforce. However, the characterology of these variables is dissimilar. They also differ in their significance for adjustment to work. Caste is an ascribed characteristic, which is decided even while in embryo. Education, skill, and training, on the other hand, are the principal achieved status attributes. Income levels form one of the bases of social gradation in both the traditional and the industrial societies. Caste by itself may have no significance in workers' adjustment to the new order, but its influence may show up because of its association with such social attributes as education and economic status. In traditional Indian society, the lower caste status of a person is very likely to be associated with lower levels of education and income.

With the spreading of education to villages and the hinterland—as has happened during the last two decades—,the younger people in the lower caste groups will be among the first to be pushed out in search of better prospects. Further, it is more likely that such persons will migrate to new growth centres where job competition is less severe and employment opportunities are relatively greater. On the other hand, the higher castes will show less propensity to migrate. The facts of younger age, urban origin, migratory status, and past experience of employment and unemployment are important for adjustment to the new order in the sense that they condition the workers' attitudes towards work, empathy, risk-taking, etc., and their perception of the job market. Thus, caste, education, and income are the most crucial social attributes of adjustment to work. Age, migration, dependency load (family size), and past experience of employment and unemployment are of secondary importance in the employees' adjustment to work.

The Hypotheses

The quality of labour-management relations, labour discipline, and labour productivity in an undertaking are dependent on several factors, basic among them being the ability of the workforce to adjust to the requirements of work. A management frames rules for recruitment, hours of work, working conditions, wages and the method of their payment, tenure of service, etc. It also fixes targets for individual as well as group output. Having made the rules and fixed targets, a management expects the workforce to be disciplined and conform to them. It also helps the workforce to make adjustments to the work by developing suitable policies on training of workers and supervisors, promotions and incentives, communication and suggestion schemes, housing and welfare services, etc. Nevertheless, prescribed management policies may generate varying responses from workers. One worker may be happy with the shift timings, while another may resort to frequent absenteeism. 'X' likes his working conditions, but 'Y' reacts and files complaints. Why do workers show such great variations in their response patterns and adjustment to work? What are the problems involved in human adjustment to the factory system? What factors influence human adjustment?

This study attempts to seek answers to these questions. In particular, it tests the following hypotheses.

Human adjustment to the factory system is influenced by three sets of forces operating simultaneously on the work situation. They are : the institutional factors, the job factors, and the socio-personal factors.

> (i) The most important institutional factors are the technology used in the production process, the size

and ownership of the plant, and the job status of the employees. The human adjustment to work is correlated with all the four institutional factors. Superior technology, private ownership of the company, large size of the plant, and high job status of the operative lead employees to higher adjustment to work. We expect to find that employees working in private companies of bigger size, where the production process is automated or involves machine control operations, are better adjusted to work than those working in public sector undertakings, or in assembly or processing plants of smaller size. Further, we expect to find supervisors displaying a higher degree of adjustment than workers and clerks.

(ii) An employee's adjustment to work is dependent on a positive correlation among his expectations (what the company *should* be doing for him), perceptions (what he finds the company *is* doing for him), and reactions (whether he is *satisfied* or not) to his job and its intrinsic factors. The most important intrinsic job factors are wages, employment security, opportunity for advancement, supervisors, working conditions, work group, and housing. If an employee perceives a company to be doing for him what he thinks it ought to do, his reaction to it will be favourable, and he is likely to be better adjusted to work. Thus, an employee's adjustment to work is negatively correlated with his expectation-perception discrepancy on each of the seven job factors. Stated differently, an employee's favourable reaction to his job leads him to better adjustment to work.

(iii) The social characteristics and personal attributes of employees influence their ability to make adjustment to work. We expect to find an association between adjustment to work of employees and such of their socio-personal attributes as age, educational level, income status, skill, caste, origin, migratory pattern, employment standing, and past experience of employment and unemployment. Higher education, higher income, younger age, urban background, migratory status, lower caste, lower dependency load, and longer employment standing of employees should be associated with a higher degree of adjustment to work. If socio-personal attributes of employees can be ranked according to their influence on adjustment to work, we expect to find education, income, and family size to be the primary influences, followed by the nature of the background, migratory status, and past employment experience.

THE SIGNIFICANCE OF KOTA

Kota was selected for carrying out the study. The township represents a growth pattern which is typical of most of the new industrial estates in India, and is likely to be the dominant growth pattern in future. Following the availability of hydro-electric power, and facilitated by the liberal fiscal policies of the State government, industries started coming into Kota. Barring a few, most industries were small enterprises established by new entrants to manufacturing occupations. Within a short period of five years, a small sleepy town of white-collar persons was transformed into a big city pulsating with industrial activity. Extensive construction of dams, canals, power houses, and buildings, plant fabrication, and growing industrial production created an acute shortage of unskilled as well as skilled hands, and clerks and supervisors. Large-scale immigration took place. Thus, Kota has new industries, entrepreneurs who are mostly inexperienced, and workers who are equally new to industrial occupations. Unlike the big-city worker, the Kota worker typifies the *new worker*. A study of the adjustment processes of the new worker to industrial life can help in developing suitable action to cushion the shock of industrialization to which millions of our people are going to be exposed.

THE STUDY DESIGN

The first step in designing the study involved developing the typology of factories at Kota. As will be obvious from the description in Chapter II of the Kota industries, the key variables that distinguished factories from one another were the level of technology used in the production processes, the ownership of the companies, and the size of the plants. The factories showed the following characteristics on each of the three variables.

(*i*) Technology of the production processes

    Semi-automated
    Machine controlling
    Assembly and processing
    Utilities and civic services

(*ii*) Ownership of the companies

    Private
    Public or government

(*iii*) Size of the plants

    Big—employing over 300 persons
    Small—employing less than 300 persons

These variables enabled us to group all the factories into the following four types:

(*i*) Private A ...... Semi-automated process
                           Private ownership
                           Large size

(*ii*) Public A ...... Machine controlling operations
                           Public ownership
                           Large size

(*iii*) Private B ...... Assembly and processing of raw material
                           Private ownership
                           Small size

(*iv*) Public B ...... Utilities and civic services
                           Public ownership
                           Small size

Further, each of the four factory types employed three levels of employees, *viz.*, supervisors, clerks, and workers. This gave us twelve strata of respondents as shown below.

Job status	Private A	Public A	Private B	Public B
Supervisors	1	2	3	4
Clerks	5	6	7	8
Workers	9	10	11	12

The second step in the design of the study was to develop a measure of adjustment to work. A job attitude scale was developed for the purpose. (This is discussed in Chapter V.) The crucial factors that were intrinsic to the job, as also the relevant personal and social factors that could influence employees' adjustment to work, were selected after a pilot study. Thereafter the interview schedule was finalized.

THE SAMPLING

The selection of the sample posed a problem. Preliminary inquiries revealed that there were several firms that employed a sizable labour force but were not registered with the government as factories. They were mostly either contractors' firms engaged in plant fabrication and erection, or manufacturing companies whose plants were either not ready for production or only partly in operation. Consequently, a census of industrial enterprises in Kota was taken at the beginning of the study during March-April, 1964. The investigators located 254 units with 24,321 employees on their rolls. Thirty-four firms that employed more than 50 persons each and were also at least three years old were selected for drawing the sample for the following reasons: (*i*) that a workforce of less than fifty persons tended to be an informal group requiring few work rules and little formalization of procedures; and (*ii*) that a firm might take at least three years to develop personnel policies and management practices—work rules that would condition employees' adjustment to work.

The selected firms employed a total of 4,586 persons who constituted the universe. A sample of 550 respondents was drawn for the 12 strata on the basis of a systematic stratified proportionate sampling method. The universe, sample, and the relative weightage given for each of the twelve strata are shown in Table 1.

The sample constituted 12 per cent of the universe. However, as one of the factories was not in a position to co-operate in the study, the number of respondents interviewed dropped to 462. The final stratum-wise distribution of the respondents is given in Table 2.

The attendance roll of each firm was utilized for selecting the required number of respondents. The attendance roll was divided into three parts according to the job status of the employees—workers, clerks, and supervisors. The respondents for each group were selected by the use of random numbers.

The Data Collection

The respondents were interviewed by a team of four investigators. All interviews were conducted on a Schedule (see Appendix-A) and were held at the residences of the respondents. The field work was completed during April-September, 1964, and the data refer to the workforce at the time of interview.

Another block of data pertained to the firms, such as history, growth of capital investment, employment and product, management practices, wage rates, absenteeism, labour turnover, unionism, etc., and were collected from the records of the firms concerned. Interviews were also held with several executives, managers, chiefs of personnel, and the government officers belonging to the departments of labour, industries, and statistics of the Rajasthan Government.

The survey was the first ever to be conducted at Kota by a research Centre. For many firms and most employees, this study was their first research interview experience. Naturally, they were apprehensive, if not suspicious. Impartiality, objectivity, and confidentiality on the part of the

TABLE 1

Table showing the universe, sample and the relative weightage given to each stratum

Category	A Private	A Public	B Private	B Public	Total Private	Total Public	Grand total
Workers:							
Universe	492	1160	1694	521	2186	1681	3867
Sample	60	140	203	61	263	201	464
Relative Weight	0·1073	0·253	0·369	0·1114	0·4767	0·366	0·845
Supervisors:							
Universe	59	86	169	61	228	147	375
Sample	7	10	20	8	27	18	45
Relative weight	0·013	0·0187	0·037	0·0133	0·049	0·032	0·082
Clerks:							
Universe	106	90	105	43	211	133	344
Sample	12	11	12	6	24	17	41
Relative weight	0·231	0·02	0·023	0·091	0·046	0·03	0·075
Total:							
Universe	657	1336	1968	625	2625	1961	4586
Sample	79	161	235	75	314	236	550

TABLE 2

Table showing the stratum-wise distribution of the respondents

Job status	Total	Type of factories				Nature of enterprises		Size of factories	
	All factories	Private A	Public A	Private B	Public B	Private sector	Public sector	A Type	B Type
Workers	391	60	140	130	61	190	201	200	191
Clerks	34	12	11	5	6	17	17	23	11
Supervisors	37	7	10	12	8	19	18	17	20
TOTAL	462	79	161	147	75	226	236	240	222

research team, in both practice and appearance, were scrupulously maintained. The study team set up its own office and hired living quarters near workers' residences, and did not accept cooperation and help from any firm more than what was strictly necessary. The detailed data from company sources were collected after the interviews with respondents were over. Officers of different government departments were apprised of the study and requested to vouchsafe for the research interests of the study team.

The Chapter Scheme

The study is presented in seven chapters. Chapter I presents the theoretical formulations, the concepts used, and the design and method of study. Chapter II describes the setting of the study—Kota and its factories. Social characteristics of the workforce are presented in Chapter III. The impact of the Kota factory system on the attitudes and perceptions of its workforce has been discussed under the title 'In the Job Market' and is the subject-matter of Chapter IV. The analysis of employees' adjustment to work and the factors influencing the adjustment have been presented in Chapter V. Chapter VI deals with the employees' image of work, which is based on the expectations, perceptions, and reactions analysis of job factors. The implications of the results of the study for theory as well as for practice have been brought out in Chapter VII. This is followed by appendices which include a section on 'The Construction Worker' which constituted a sub-section of the main investigation, schedules used in the study, a select bibliography, and an index.

Chapter II

KOTA AND ITS FACTORIES

Introduction

KOTA was one of the 20 princely States that were integrated in 1956 to constitute the present State of Rajasthan. Currently, it is one of the 26 districts of Rajasthan covering an area of 12,450 square kilometres[1] in the extreme south-eastern part of the State. Unlike most other parts of the State, this district has rich and productive table lands irrigated by the Chambal river and its tributaries. The area abounds in thick forest products, building material, glass sand, and limestone. The climate is generally hot and dry. The rainfall averages 76·2 centimetres a year.[2]

Kota city is the district headquarters. Founded as a principality in 1342, the city was extended and granted the status of a State by the Moghuls in 1625. It became a British protectorate in 1817.[3] Today, Kota is one of the six biggest cities of Rajasthan. Situated on the right bank of the Chambal river, the city and the surrounding area have better natural gifts than the rest of the district. The strategic location, abundance of water supply, and availability of raw material make for its vast growth potential.

The city has been an administrative and commercial centre for over six hundred years. Its industrial development did not start, however, till after 1958 when the first stage of the Chambal Hydro-Electric Project was completed. Following the availability of hydro-electric power, and facilitated by the liberal industrial and fiscal policies of the State government, industries started coming into Kota. There-

---

[1] Government of India, *Census of India* 1961, Part II(A).

[2] Milap Chand Dandia (ed.), *Rajasthan Year Book and Who is Who*, Jaipur, Sammriddhi Publications, 1963.

[3] Superintendent of Government Printing, *Imperial Gazetteer of India*, Provincial Series, Rajputana, Calcutta, 1908.

after, rapid industrial development took place, which brought significant changes in the social and demographic contours of the area.

Demographic Changes

The population of Kota district rose from 670,060 in 1951[4] to 848,389 in 1961,[5] registering an increase of 178 thousand. The population of Kota city was recorded at 37·8 thousand in 1931, 47·3 thousand in 1941, 65·1 thousand in 1951, and 120·1 thousand in 1961.[6] In 1963-64, it was estimated at about 150 thousand. During the period 1951-1961, the annual growth rate of the city was 8·48 per cent against 2·66 for the Kota district and 2·62 for Rajasthan.[7] A comparison of the occupational distribution of the workforce at the three levels brings out sharp differences. In 1961, 1·79 and 2·37 per cent[8] of the workforce were employed in manufacturing industries in the State and Kota district respectively. The corresponding percentage for Kota city worked out at approximately 32·5 in June 1963.[9] During the census decade 1951-1961, the percentage of urban population in the district rose from 16·72 to 18·69,[10] and the literacy rate increased from 12·19 to 19·05 per cent.[11]

A vegetable oil mill was the first industrial enterprise to be set up at Kota in 1908. Much of the industrial activity during the next five decades concerned itself with the processing of the local produce, and quarrying of lime, sand, and glass sand. Thermal power generation was started in 1926, followed by the city water supply system in 1929. A small plant that manufactured pilfer-proof seals

---

[4] Government of India, *Census of India* 1951, Vol. I, Part II(A).

[5] Government of India, *Census of India* 1961, Vol. I, Part II-A(i).

[6] *Ibid.*

[7] *Rajasthan Year Book and Who is Who*, opp. cit.

[8] Government of India, *Census of India* 1961, Paper No. 1, 1962, Appendix I.

[9] Calculated: Total workforce in Kota was taken from the 1961 Census. Persons employed in manufacturing industries were taken from the report of Employment Exchange, 2nd., Quarterly, 1963.

[10] *Census of India* 1951 and 1961, opp. cit.

[11] Directorate of Economics and Statistics, Jaipur, Rajasthan, *Basic Statistics*, 1960 and 1963.

and crowns for bottles was set up in 1942 by a Parsi merchant from Bombay. The Chambal Workshop came into existence in 1952, and the Wagon Repair Workshop in 1957. A private, medium size cotton spinning mill started working the same year. Thus far, apart from quarrying and oil pressing activity, Kota city had three factories in the private sector, two workshops in the public sector, and the public utilities.

As has been stated earlier, rapid industrialization started after 1958. One of the biggest PVC manufacturing plants in India, and a chemical plant to manufacture rayon yarn came into existence in 1960. A large number of assembly and processing factories made their appearance in the next two years. In 1963, Kota had 235 registered factories (of varying ages) each employing more than 50 persons, in 12 of which women workers constituted 9.61 per cent.[12]

Corresponding changes took place in other spheres of the city's life. Supply and consumption of electricity increased significantly. In 1958, the total supply and consumption of power was 3.65 and 2.69 million kilowatts[13] respectively. In December 1962, the corresponding figures stood at 22.81 and 20.68 million kilowatts.[14] The available road mileage in the Kota district went up from 997 to 1,110 during the period 1958-1962.[15] The number of motorized vehicles rose from 1,602 to 3,300 during the same period.[16] The number of schools and colleges in the district went up from 523 in 1957-58 to 1,139 in 1961-62; and the number of pupils from 44,277 to 83,886.[17] Four technical training institutes were established during 1958-1961. Three of them trained carpenters, electricians, wire men, fitters, surveyors, blacksmiths, block and die makers,

---

[12] Compiled from the Quarterly Reports (1963-64) of the Employment Exchange, Kota, Rajasthan.

[13] Directorate of Economics and Statistics, Jaipur, Rajasthan, *Statistical Abstract*, 1959.

[14] *Ibid.*, 1962

[15] *Ibid.*, 1959 and 1962.

[16] Records: Office of the District Transport and Registering Authority, Kota, Rajasthan.

[17] *Statistical Abstract*, opp. cit., 1958 and 1962.

printers, foot-wear makers, etc. The fourth institute imparted a three-year diploma course in electrical, mechanical, and civil engineering.

The Nature of Industry

The above account of Kota points out to a very important fact. The Kota district in general, and Kota city in particular, have been undergoing rapid social change due to the industrialization and the resultant urbanization. A large number of factories came into existence in a relatively short period of five years. A survey of these factories brought out sharp inter-factory differences on key variables.

First, they differed in the level of technology that determined the relationship of man to machine, and skill requirements. Two chemical plants had continuous manufacturing processes and were, by and large, automated. A few high skilled personnel were required to control the 'mix' of raw material, set the pace of the process, adjust the temperature and pressure, and to ensure the required quality control. Low skilled persons were employed on ancillary and subsidiary operations. Then, there were workshops engaged in tool and die making, and in the maintenance of machines. They required skilled workers who could individually direct machines and control their operations. The resultant work organization involved a skilled worker to operate the machine and one or more helpers with lesser or no skills.

There were also a large number of processing and assembly plants. Here, work operation involved the input of semi-finished or semi-processed goods that were converted into finished marketable products. It required a number of individual operatives clustered by the type of machines they tended and the nature of the product of the machines. Each operative was required to possess technical know-how of only one operation nn the machine and to perform it repetitively. Finally, there were utilities such as electricity and water supply services where worker performance required little skill. Most workers were required to possess some minimal experience of doing a job which came to its peak quickly at a low level and then levelled off. The work was performed in gangs. The only recognized skills involved machine maintenance and ability to work with complicated machines, and these were at the supervisory level.

Second, the factories differed in the nature of ownership. The basic difference was between the public and the private sectors. The public sector undertakings belonged either to the State or to the Central government. In these undertakings, the rule-making authorities were not local, and the rules were made for all the employees, of which the Kota groups were only one part. The local authorities had to fit themselves into the broad national or regional patterns. The undertakings were not run for private profit, and were less flexible to local considerations.

The third important variable was the size of the plants in terms of employment. Four factories employed more than 300 persons each. They had well-established reporting relationships, clear supervisory patterns, formal personnel policies, and a functional bureaucratic set-up. The other factories did not formalize the hierarchical relationship within the organization. Non-applicability of most of the basic labour laws and lax inspections contributed to the non-formalization of managerial practices in such factories.

A detailed description of the factories is given below.

Chemical Plants

Both the chemical plants were established in 1960. The bigger of the two produces PVC powder that is used in a variety of secondary and tertiary industries. The second plant makes synthetic rayon fibre and converts it into yarn which is despatched to sister concerns for weaving cloth. Both factories are owned by corporations that also hold a variety of manufacturing interests all over the country. The controlling parties—the managing agents—are third generation industrialists in both cases. All the managers and most of the other senior executives came to Kota on transfer from the parent body or the sister units. The philosophy of industrial management, the patterns of organizational structure, management and personnel practices, the perception of management's role in industry, etc., that the employers and managers brought with them influenced the development of the management practices of the local units.

The management of the rayon fibre plant was unable to cooperate in the study due to unavoidable reasons. Detailed information was available for the PVC plant only.

Construction work on the sixty million rupee PVC plant started in April 1962 and was completed in June 1964. Though production started in late 1963, the plant came into full operation in 1964 only. The average daily employment in 1962 was reported to be about 3,000 construction workers, and 40 production staff. In April 1964, the average daily employment was 657 production and 252 construction employees. The best amongst the large pool of construction workers engaged in plant erection were selected for employment on production work. Most of the clerks were recruited from the local market. Supervisors were recruited by the personnel department of the managing agency which has access to a wider labour market in all parts of the country. The monthly rates of wages paid by the company were relatively higher as compared to those paid by other companies in the area. The company rates are shown below.

Workers
  Skilled   ..   Rs. 150 to 450
  Semi-skilled/Unskilled   ..   Rs. 110 to 200
Clerks   ..   Rs. 200 to 400
Supervisors   ..   Rs. 300 to 1000

The factory preferred to hire persons with readily usable skills, and has well-developed recruitment policy and selection procedures. It maintained higher wage rates, well-defined reporting relationships, clearly stated workloads, and formal rules regarding hours of work and working conditions. The enterprise had no housing or training schemes at the time of the study. Promotion policy was not formally stated, but annual assessment of employee performance was done and merit was rewarded by promotion.

Tool Manufacturing Plant

The Wagon Repair Workshop belongs to the Railway Board, Government of India. The workshop was set up in 1957 to repair wagons. The tool-making operations were added in 1960, and the manufacture of rolling stock was started in 1964. The capital investment and employment in the workshop grew with the increase in its activities. The capital investment rose from 1,100 thousand rupees in 1960 to 1,170 thousand rupees in 1964. The employment increased from 387 to 1,539 during the same period. The manager and many other senior executives of the workshop are senior engineering personnel of the Indian Railway Service. All employees are transferable to other railway establishments outside Kota. Supervisors, clerks, and skilled workers are recruited by a selection board. Unskilled workers, who are mostly temporary, can be recruited locally. Civil service rules as applicable to the Railways are followed for purposes of recruitment and selection. Promotions are based on seniority within the same slab. Slab jumping is linked with training, and a training institute is attached to the workshop. Low quit rate, the policy of determining seniority on the basis of an occupational category throughout the organization (Railway Board), and of filling vacancies by transferring employees from other stations have resulted in limited opportunities for promotion. A housing estate is also attached to the workshop. Initially, all employees were provided with residential accommodation. However, the rate of growth of the workforce has been faster than the rate of house building activity and only half of the operatives had been provided with living quarters by April 1964. A Works Committee and three joint committees—for canteen, safety, and sports—operate in the workshop.

The following monthly rates of wages were prevalent at the time of the study.

Workers
  Skilled   .. Rs. 175 to 240
  Semi-skilled   .. Rs. 75 to 110
  Unskilled   .. Rs. 70 to 80
Clerks   .. Rs. 175 to 425
Supervisors   .. Rs. 150 to 575

The above account establishes that this plant also had well-developed personnel practices regarding recruitment, selection, and training of employees. Promotions were based on occupational seniority. The housing colony accommodated about half of the workforce on low rentals. Wage rates for workers and clerks were comparable to those of their counterparts in 'Private A', but were low for supervisors. Rules regarding job security were very favourable to employees. Joint consultation was in vogue, and the workforce was adequately unionized.

Assembly and Processing

The factories of this type employed up to 300 persons, are engaged in assembly or processing work, and are owned by either partnership firms or private limited companies (the only exception being a public limited company). All of them were family enterprises and differed only in the legal form of organization. All excepting two were established after 1958. The following list indicates the nature of some of the more important manufacturing processes in which they were engaged:

Oil crushing, vanaspati, and acids.
Spinning cotton or cotton and rayon waste.
Rayon yarn, wool thread.
Metal pressing.
Steel furniture.
Wool tops.
Strawboard.
Brass and steel wires.
Wires and conduits.
Sulphur containers.
Crowns for bottles and containers.
Air compressors.
Radio parts and radio assembly.
Polythene toys and tops.
Hard metal tools.
Forging and casting.
Foundry.
Auto parts.

Most of the enterprises underwent rapid growth during 1960-1964. The growth in capital investment and manpower in eight units for which data were available is shown below.

Unit No.	Capital Investment (Unit : lakh rupees) April 1960	1964	Workforce April 1960	1964
1.	2·00	5·25	150	204
2.	3·62	8·00	15	165
3.	3·20	8·00	132	229
4.	2·65	2·65	25	250
5.	2·00	3·50	20	250
6.	0·32	0·37	30	103
7.	5·00	7·50	64	143
8.	0·30	1·05	16	172

Except one entrepreneur, all were new to manufacturing activity, and belonged to traders' families. Only two of them originated from Rajasthan, and the rest moved in from Bombay, Delhi, and the Punjab.

A common characteristic of all enterprises of this type is the absence of formally defined policies and procedures. Recruitment, grant of wage increments, and discharge, etc., were done informally and on an *ad hoc* basis. Generally the manager was a member of the controlling interest and he placed great reliance on one or more supervisors who were considered indispensable. The authority was vested in these two levels of functionaries (manager and supervisors selected by him). No other formal reporting relationships or representative structures existed in the organizations. Wage rates paid to employees compared unfavourably with those in 'Private A'. The following range of monthly wages was found to be prevalent.

Workers
   Skilled   ..   Rs.   80 to 200
   Semi-skilled   ..   Rs.   44 to 150
   Unskilled   ..   Rs.   38 to   90
Clerks   ..   Rs.   90 to 150
Supervisors   ..   Rs. 110 to 500

From the foregoing discussion we find that the 'Private B' type factories were less formalized organizations; employees worked under conditions of undefined work rules, job insecurity, and low wage rates. The entrepreneurs were new to manufacturing activity. They placed great reliance on a few selected supervisors, held on to them, and cared little for other employees.

Utilities and Services

This type included public utilities, such as water supply, power distribution, buildings and maintenance of roads, parks and dams, etc. They belonged to the State government, and are analogous to government departments in their structure and functions. Formerly, most of these undertakings belonged to the princely States, and the employees were integrated into the respective regular cadres of Rajasthan. The new State inherited services that were over-staffed by persons not always selected on merit. During the period 1960-1964, whereas the local workforce in the Public Works Department (buildings, roads, etc.), water works, and the State workshop decreased, primarily due to rationalization of staff, it went up from 143 to 432 in the State Electricity Board and from 438 to 640 in the canal maintenance wing of the Public Works Department.

All organizations of this type were headed by engineers that are employees of the State government and could be transferred within its territorial jurisdiction. Service conditions of employees in all units were regulated by the State civil service rules. Fresh hands were recruited to the bottom level jobs. Vacancies at all other levels were filled in by moving up the senior most employees from the immediately lower level. The following monthly wage scales operated in all organizations.

Workers
    Skilled   .. Rs. 110 to 180
    Semi-skilled   .. Rs. 75 to 110
    Unskilled   .. Rs. 70 to 80
Clerks   .. Rs. 90 to 340
Supervisors   .. Rs. 115 to 330

To sum up, the presentation on the foregoing pages portrays a situation which is typical of many growth centres in the country. In the case of Kota, a hydro-electric power plant came into existence near a small town. Power attracted industry. Heavy industrial plants were followed by secondary and tertiary industries. The traditional commercial and administrative centre began growing into an industrial metropolis. The next six years witnessed enormous quantitative and qualitative changes in the township. The town doubled its population. Over 250 industrial enterprises employing about 24,000 workers came into existence. This introduced changes in the composition of the population, occupational patterns, and levels of education and income. Electricity consumption, road mileage, motorized vehicles, schools, colleges, and technical training institutes increased rapidly.

The inflow of technology and manufacturing activity in the town telescoped the process of social change, and gave direction to it. Plants differed in their use of technology, size, and ownership. These differences introduced variations in work organization, reporting relationships, skill requirement, and social quality of the workforce in the plants. Thus, the technology not only initiated social change in the area but also was responsible for qualitative differentiations in the workforce, as we shall see in the subsequent chapters.

Chart showing characteristics of plants by factory types

(1)	Private A (2)	Public A (3)	Private B (4)	Public B (5)
1. Product	PVC, Chemicals, Synthetics	Manufacture and repair of railway rolling stock, tool making.	Extraction of oils and processing, metal pressing, steel furniture, cotton spinning, wire making and insulation, radio parts and assembly, air compressors, forging, casting, hard metal tools, auto parts. Assembly and processing.	Construction of buildings and roads, maintenance of dams, canals and roads, water supply, electricity distribution, work shops.
2. Manufacturing process	Semi-automatic, continuous	Intermittent, machine controlling.	Machine tending operations by a group, individual's role unidentifiable.	Public utilities.
3. Role of operatives	Setting pace to the process, adjustment of inputs, quality control, etc.	Machine control operation, quality of output of a machine determined by the skill of its operators.		Gang labour, recognised skills at supervisory level only.
4. Ownership	Owned by private corporations and run for purposes of profits	Public owned.	Owned by small partnership firms or private limited concerns, run for profit making.	Owned by the State government for service to the community, non-profit making.
5. Size: Average daily employment	More than 500 persons	More than 500 persons.	Between 100 and 300 persons.	Between 100 and 300 persons.
Capital Investment	60 million rupees (one unit only)	Rs. 1170 thousand.	Varied from 30 to 160 thousand rupees.	Not available.
6. Recruitment Workers	Local market	Locally for temporary hands. Centrally by the parent body for all other positions.	Local market.	Local market.
Clerks	Mostly local		Mostly local.	Local.

(1)	(2)	(3)	(4)	(5)
Supervisors	All over the country	Do.	Mostly from non-local market.	Local.
7. Selection procedure	Formal	Formal.	Informal.	Formal.
8. Promotions	On merit basis, ad hoc policy	On seniority basis, formal policy.	Not practised.	On seniority basis, formal policy.
9. Joint plant committees	Did not exist	Four committees functioned.	Did not exist.	Did not exist.
10. Grievance handling	No formal policy	Formal policy.	No policy.	Civil service rules applied.
11. Housing	Not provided	Half of employees provided with houses, more being built.	Not provided.	Provided to the essential staff only.
12. Fringe benefits	None	Dearness allowance, provident fund, credit facilities, gratuity.	Not provided.	Dearness allowance, provident fund.
13. Welfare services	As per Factories Act, 1948.	As per Factories Act, 1948.	None.	None.
14. Leaves, hours of work, working conditions	As per Factories Act, 1948.	As per Factories Act, 1948.	Generally as per Factories Act, 1948.	As per civil service rules for industrial employees.
15. Wages (Rs. p.m.):				
Workers:				
Skilled	150-450	175-240	80-200	110-180
Semi-skilled	110-200	75-110	44-150	75-110
Unskilled	90-90	70-80	38-70	70-80
Clerks	200-400	175-424	90-150	90-340
Supervisors	300-1000	150-575	110-500	115-330

CHAPTER III

SOCIAL CHARACTERISTICS OF THE WORKFORCE

SLOTKIN stated that 'new industrial employees become available from among those people who find their traditional culture inadequate'.[1] If we were to agree with him, it might be expected that the new workforce would be drawn from economically marginal groups or from lower castes or would have migrated from areas where traditional occupations were uneconomic. One might also expect the young and educated migrants from rural areas to make up a disproportionately larger segment of the workforce. Considering all such possibilities, Lambert said, 'One would not expect the factory workforce to be a representative cross-section of the surrounding society on those social characteristics which counted most in fixing a man's status... one would anticipate that recruitment would be socially selective.'[2] In this chapter, we shall consider the social characteristics of our sample from the viewpoint of the cultural inadequacy and social selectivity concepts of Slotkin and Lambert. This will be done by comparing the social characteristics of the sample with those of the populations of Kota district and Rajasthan. Further, a comparison of the social attributes of respondents by factory types and job status will be made. This will help us to understand the influence of the institutional framework on their adjustment to work. The data are given at the end of the chapter and references made at appropriate places.

AGE

Table 1 shows that 63·4 per cent of respondents were less than 30 years old, 24·0 per cent in the age group of 30-40,

---
[1] J.S. Slotkin, *From Field to Factory*, p.33.
[2] R.D. Lambert, *Factories, Workers and Social Change in India*, pp.22-23.

and 12·6 per cent more than 40 years old. A break-up by job status reveals that 64·2 per cent of workers, 70·6 per cent of clerks, and 48·6 per cent of supervisors were below 30 years. Twenty-seven per cent of supervisors were more than 40 years old against 5·8 per cent of clerks and 11·8 per cent of workers. A comparison of the age of respondents by factory types (Table 2) brings out that the younger-age respondents constituted the overwhelming majority of the workforce in private enterprises. A comparison by factory types shows that 84·8 per cent respondents in 'Private A' and 67·3 per cent in 'Private B' factories were less than 30 years old against 58·4 and 43·9 per cent respectively in 'Public A' and 'Public B' factories. The 'Public B' type had the largest proportion of employees who were more than 40 years old. A break-up of respondents' age by factory types and job status (Table 3) confirms further that the workforce in private enterprises was younger than that of public undertakings; and that clerks were younger than workers and supervisors. It also shows that, 'Private A' type had the largest percentage of youngest employees.

The fact that respondents in the public sector undertakings were older than those in the private enterprises might not be a function of recruitment but of seniority-based promotion policy and better provisions of job security in the former category. Public sector undertakings were older in age and had a lower rate of turnover resulting in a larger number of employees having longer periods of service with their companies.

Literacy and Level of Education

The literacy rate for the sample—as worked out—was 76·0 per cent against 19·05 per cent for Kota district and 15·21 per cent for Rajasthan. If clerks and supervisors are excluded, the literacy rate for the workers' group alone would be 71·9 per cent. The factory workforce at Kota was nearly five times more literate than the population of Rajasthan and four times more literate than those residing in the district. The literacy rate for 'A' type factories was 84·3 per cent against 67·6 per cent for 'B' type and 83·1 per cent for public undertakings against 68·8 per cent for private enterprises. Further, 'Public A' type had the highest literacy rate (90·1 per cent) followed by 'Private A' (78·5 per cent), 'Public B' (75·0 per cent), and 'Private B' (59·2 per cent). Thus, the literacy rate was higher in bigger size factories and also in public undertakings.

The data regarding the levels of education of the population of Rajasthan and Kota district are not available for comparison. Of our sample, 24·0 per cent had no schooling, 52·4 per cent had pre-high school education, and the remaining 23·6 per cent were educated beyond high school. As education would have been an important consideration for recruiting all clerks and most supervisors, an analysis of the level of education of workers would be more revealing. Of the workers' group, 28·1 per cent had no schooling, 16·6 per cent had education beyond high school, and the remaining 55·3 per cent had pre-high school education. Illiteracy was the highest amongst workers in 'Private B' type (45·4 per cent) and the lowest in 'Public A' type (11·4 per cent). Thirty per cent workers in 'Private A' were educated beyond high school in contrast to 2·2 per cent in 'Private B' type where 8·3 per cent supervisors were also illiterate. Thus we find that the factory workforce had a very high rate of literacy as compared to that of the district and the State. The rate was higher in bigger size factories and in public sector undertakings. The lowest level of education was found in 'Private B' type. All supervisors and clerks, and 30·0 per cent workers in 'Private A' type were educated beyond high school. The public undertakings were characterized by higher literacy rate but medium level of education of all employees—workers, clerks, and supervisors.

Skill

All supervisors and clerks were skilled persons by definition, and therefore the analysis was confined to workers only. Of the total workers, 51·6 per cent were unskilled,[3]

---

[8]In order to arrive at a standard and uniform pattern of workers' classification by skill, an inventory of job designations for all factories was made. Thereafter, each job designation was assigned one of the three skill categories.

27·2 per cent were semi-skilled, and the remaining 21·2 per cent were skilled. Forty-five per cent workers in 'Private A' type were unskilled compared to 27·0 per cent in 'Public A'. The 'B' type factories employed unskilled workers in larger proportion. Sixty-eight and 64·0 per cent of workers in 'Private B' and 'Public B' types respectively were unskilled. The percentage of skilled workers was the highest in 'Public A' (41·0) and the lowest in 'Private B' (1·0). An analysis of unskilled workers according to their migratory status revealed that local workers were more unskilled than the migrants. In 'Private A', 22·0 per cent of the migrants were unskilled. The corresponding figures were 3·0 per cent in 'Public A', 76·0 per cent in 'Private B', and 40·0 per cent in 'Public B'.

Background and Migration

The data pertaining to the background and the migration of respondents are presented in Tables 7 and 8. Table 7 shows that 55·0 per cent of respondents came from rural areas. Compared to this, 81·31 per cent of the workforce of Kota district, and 83·7 per cent of that of Rajasthan belonged to rural areas. This shows that the Kota workforce was less rural in background than that of the Kota district and the State. A comparison of the background of respondents by factory types shows that 28·0 per cent of workers in 'Private A' were from urban areas as compared to 62·0 per cent in 'Public B'. This may be due to the fact that 80·0 per cent of the employees of 'Public B' belonged to Kota city. On the other hand, 'Private A' employed 33·0 per cent local workers.

Fifty-five per cent of respondents in 'Public A' type were immigrants from other States. The corresponding figures for other factory types were, 8·0 per cent for 'Public B' and 40·0 per cent each for 'Private A' and 'Private B'. In view of the fact that employees in 'Public A' were subject to transfer on an all-India basis, a higher percentage of immigrants from other States is not surprising. 'Public B' included civil services of the former princely State of

Kota. Therefore, it is equally less surprising if very few immigrants are to be found in that. However, the proportion of immigrant respondents in private enterprises is significant.

Caste

Does the social organization of the community get reflected in the social structure of the workforce? The data revealed interesting trends.

Of the total sample, 41·4 per cent were Harijans, 10·6 per cent Vaishyas, and 24·1 and 23·8 per cent Kshatriyas and Brahmins respectively. The caste structure of Kota city, Kota district, and Rajasthan was not available; hence no comparison could be made. All the same, it seems unlikely that the percentage of Harijans in the general population or even in the workforce in the district or the State could be as high. This indicates that industry attracted Harijans more than other caste groups. A classification of respondents by job status reveals that Harijans constituted 46·1 per cent of workers, 6·9 per cent of supervisors, and 22·5 per cent of clerks. Brahmins constituted 24·3 per cent of workers, 13·8 per cent of supervisors, and 28·1 per cent of clerks. Harijans constituted the largest single caste group amongst workers, and Vaishyas amongst supervisors. The clerks' group was constituted almost equally by all the four castes. It was also found that about 90·0 per cent of Harijans in all factory types came to Kota either from other districts of Rajasthan or from other States. The caste structure of the workforce at Kota showed that the higher castes could obtain higher jobs in better factories in larger proportions. No factory recruited its workforce on the caste basis. Therefore, it could be surmised that the caste structure of the workforce was the outcome of various social forces. If we were to examine the districts of origin and family occupations of migrant workers, it might be found that the economic status of the respondents and the condition of agricultural land were strong factors of 'push' to Kota.

Family Size and Composition

The average family size of the respondents worked out at 5·12 against 5·8 for Kota district and 6·35 for Rajasthan. The industrial workforce at Kota had a relatively smaller family compared to the population in the district and in Rajasthan. Table 11 shows that family size was the largest in 'Private A' and the smallest in 'Private B'. An analysis of family size by job status of respondents shows that supervisors had bigger size families (5·78) than workers (4·90) or clerks (4·69). Supervisors in 'Private A' had the largest average family (8·14).

Table 12 presents the economic status of the members of respondents' families. It was observed that the average number of earners in clerks' families was higher than in those of workers and supervisors (1·64 against 1·44 for workers and 1·48 for supervisors). The number of dependents per earner was also the lowest amongst the clerks' group (1·85 for clerks, 2·4 for workers, and 2·9 for supervisors). It was mentioned earlier that clerks had the smallest size families as well. Considered by factory types, it was noticed that though the average number of earners per family was the highest in 'Private A' (1·75), the dependency load per earner was the lowest in 'Private B'. It ('Private B') had 2·1 dependents per earner against 2·39 in 'Private A', 3·1 in 'Public A', and 2·23 in 'Public B'.

The survey also revealed that the majority of married clerks had working wives. Being younger in age and of local origin, most of them lived in joint families and were relatively free from many of the family responsibilities. Most of the supervisors were migrants and heads of their families who in turn were primarily dependent on them.

Income

The average monthly family income of the respondents worked out at Rs. 272·66. Table 13 shows the family income of the respondents by their job status and factory types. The average monthly family income of workers was Rs. 144·79, of clerks Rs. 219·15, and of supervisors

Rs. 452·26. The respondents' monthly income was the highest in 'Private A' for all the three job status groups and the lowest in 'Private B' except for supervisors, whose income was higher than those of 'Public B'. The family income of supervisors in 'Private A' was considerably higher than that of supervisors from other types of factories.

The monthly average per capita income of the respondents was Rs. 53·25. The corresponding figures for the workforce in Kota district and Rajasthan were Rs. 34·35 and Rs. 19·92 respectively. This indicates that the industrial workforce at Kota was much better off than workers either in the surrounding area or in the State.

Take-home pay indicates the amount actually available to an employee for spending. An analysis of workers' take-home pay was done to find out inter-factory differences. This is presented in Table 14. We find that the percentage of workers falling in the group 'less than Rs. 100 per month' was the lowest in respect of 'Private A' (32·9), and the highest in 'Private B' (65·3). In 'Private A', 17·8 per cent of workers earned take-home pay exceeding Rs. 200 per month compared to 3·7 per cent in 'Public A', 4·1 per cent in 'Private B', and 6·6 per cent in 'Public B'. Thus, it was found that 'Private A' had the highest wage rates.

An analysis was also done to find out the relationship between levels of income and the migratory status of persons in the workers' group only. The results are presented in Table 15. It was found that, apart from 3·0 per cent of workers in 'Private B', no local worker earned more than Rs. 200 per month. Fifty-five per cent of local workers in 'Private A', 67·0 per cent in 'Public A', 97·0 per cent in 'Private B', and 63·0 per cent in 'Public B' earned less than Rs. 100 per month. It is evident from this that the majority of local workers earned less than Rs. 100 a month and most of the immigrants between Rs. 100 and 200 per month. The relationship between the levels of income and the levels of education of local workers was also traced in 'Private A' and 'Private B', having the highest and the lowest wage rates respectively. Table 16 shows that the local workers who were educated up to and beyond high school had simi-

Occupational Changes

Table 17 shows that 46·0 per cent of respondents had no previous employer. To them the current job was the first employment experience involving supervised work, time schedules, machine operations, etc. Another 34·0 per cent had only one employer prior to the current one. Only 8·0 per cent had held three or more jobs previously. Job mobility amongst respondents was not high and the average of previous employers was only 0·9. Table 18 shows the nature of earlier jobs held by respondents. Only 9·0 per cent of the earlier jobs involved work in agriculture. 'Non-agricultural labour' accounted for 37·0 per cent of the total earlier jobs, and another 30·0 per cent were in 'technical and mechanical' occupations. Ten per cent of the earlier jobs were in civil services.

A comparison by factory types of previous jobs held by respondents brought out that only 27·0 and 25·0 per cent in 'Private A' and 'Private B' respectively had no previous employers. The corresponding percentages stood at 68·0 and 60·0 in 'Public A' and 'Public B' respectively. Similarly, the percentage of respondents who had held one job prior to the current one was two times higher in private enterprises than in public undertakings. It was also noted that 15·0 per cent of respondents in 'Private B' had held three jobs each before taking up the current employment. A similar comparison of the occupations in which previous jobs were held shows that farming accounted for 10·0 to 11·0 per cent of jobs in all factory types excepting 'Private A', where it was only 5·0 per cent. 'Technical and mechanical' occupations accounted for the largest group of respondents in 'Private A' and 'Public B'. Forty-two per cent of earlier jobs of respondents in

'Public A' and 'Private B' were held in 'non-agricultural labour' occupations.

Table 19 gives a comparison of the respondents' previous job occupations with those of their fathers. We find that fathers of 42·0 per cent of respondents were cultivators, but only 9·0 per cent of the latter had worked on the land. However, 37·0 per cent of respondents and 5·0 per cent of fathers had worked as non-agricultural labourers. Again, 30·0 per cent of the previous jobs of respondents were held in 'technical/mechanical' occupations; but fathers of only 4·0 per cent ever performed this work. Further, 'civil services' and 'trade and commerce' accounted for 10·0 per cent and 2·0 per cent respectively of respondents' previous jobs against 25·0 per cent and 8·0 per cent of fathers who fell in these categories.

A few points become clear from Tables 17, 18, and 19. First, the respondents represented a workforce a very large proportion of which was new to organized employment. Second, though a sizable portion (42·0 per cent) of respondents came from peasant stock, very few of them (9·0 per cent) had actually worked on the land. Third, the earlier job occupations of the majority of respondents were either 'technical/mechanical' (30·0 per cent) or 'non-agricultural labour' (37·0 per cent). It seems that employees in their quest for jobs moved to factories where their existing skills could be utilized. Non-agricultural labour mostly took up unskilled jobs; technical hands became skilled operatives and supervisors. Fourth, private enterprises employed more of experienced hands, but public undertakings looked for new entrants to the labour force. This difference occurred as the latter were willing to take greater responsibility for the training of raw hands. Relatively lower wages and longer time-scales of pay in public undertakings attracted more fresh men who perceived therein opportunities to move up in the plant hierarchy. Finally, 'Private A' drew a larger percentage of its workforce from 'technical/mechanical' occupations as compared to other factory types. Higher pay was the major attraction to workers as we shall see in the subsequent section.

Income Changes

Table 21 shows the distribution of the workers' group by the highest take-home pay earned in any previous job. It will be observed from the table that no worker ever took home more than Rs. 200 per month. Sixty-eight per cent took home less than one hundred rupees and the remaining 32·0 per cent between Rs. 100 and 200 per month. Relatively, more workers employed in 'Private A' and 'Public B' took home Rs. 100-200 per month. Table 22 brings out the differences in the highest ever take-home pay from the previous job and the take-home pay from the current employment of respondents. We find that on the whole, more workers took home more money now than in their previous jobs. The size of the income group of 'less than Rs. 100' decreased from 68·0 to 48·0 per cent, and that of 'Rs. 100-200' increased from 32·0 to 44·0 per cent, and 8·0 per cent workers took home more than Rs. 200 per month against none in this group in the previous jobs. Income changes were substantial for workers employed in 'Private A'. The size of the lowest take-home pay group in this type was reduced by 25·0 per cent, and 18·0 per cent of workers earned more than Rs. 200 per month for the first time. Thus, we find that the current jobs of workers gave them better income status than any of their previous jobs. The income changes were the highest in 'Private A' and the lowest in 'Public B'.

Reasons for Job Changes

The reasons that led respondents to change jobs have been presented in Table 23. Forty-five per cent of the total job changes were due to their search for 'higher wages', Fifty-seven per cent of job changes of employees in 'Private A' were assigned this reason which was also the highest amongst all factory types. Thus, wages were the principal consideration in job changes. This conclusion finds support from Table 21 where it may be noted that income status improved with change of jobs. Involuntary job changes constituted 29·0 per cent of the total. The reasons included under this category were 'closure of employing agency', conflict with supervisors, and termination of service. These reasons were given by the respondents in all factory types. The remaining 14·0 per cent job changes were due to personal and physical reasons such as ill health or family circumstances or the work place being too far away from the native place. On the whole, the search for higher wages was the most predominant reason for job changes, followed by involuntary quits and resignations due to 'family reasons'.

Unemployment

The data on respondents' unemployment are presented in Tables 24, 25, and 26. We observe from Table 24 that 42·4 per cent respondents reported no unemployment ever. It has been mentioned earlier that 46·0 per cent of the total respondents never held a job previously (Table 17). Moreover, 81·8 per cent of employees in 'Private A' and 46·7 per cent in 'Private B' suffered no unemployment. These groups also had a relatively higher rate of job changes (Table 17) and predominance of technical/mechanical background (Table 18). Thus, a lower incidence of unemployment was found to be associated with 'technical/mechanical' family backgrounds and a greater job mobility of respondents. Only 20·0 per cent employees in 'Public 'A' reported no unemployment. Considering that most of them took up their current employment at a relatively young age, and 68·0 per cent held no job earlier (Table 17), it seems that this factory drew its workforce preponderantly from persons who, while regarding themselves as having suffered unemployment, had in fact no previous job experience. Further, unemployment spells were of less than a year's duration. Table 25 shows that 63·0 per cent respondents stayed on in the local labour market during their unemployment period, 31·0 per cent returned to their native places, and only 6·0 per cent migrated to other places in search of jobs. This shows that during unemployment, the predominant tendency among respondents was to stay on and look for a job in the same area. This was facilitated by shorter spells of unemployment in the majority of cases. It is difficult to say whether they placed higher confidence in the local job market or found it more expensive to shift to a new place. The sources of subsistence during unemployment are obvious from Table 26 which shows that only 9·0 per cent respondents could live on their past savings during unemployment. Sixty-two per cent became dependents of their friends and relatives, 8·0 per cent had to borrow money, and 21·0 per cent undertook to do casual work. In 'Private A', 28·0 per cent respondents lived during unemployment on savings. On the other hand, casual work was resorted to by the majority of employees in 'Private B' during unemployment. The dominant pattern of adjusting to unemployment (by all employees) was to stay on in the local labour market and look for a job. During this period they depended on friends and relatives for maintenance.

The above presentation throws light on such demographic characteristics of the workforce of Kota as age, literacy and levels of education, skill, caste, origin, size and composition of family, income, migration, and occupational history. The factory workforce has been compared with the general workforce of Kota and Rajasthan in its social characteristics, as also by the factory type they were employed in. In view of the scarcity of empirical data on factory workforce in the new growth centres, these substantive details are of considerable interest to industrial sociologists, public policy makers, and company executives.

The analysis brings out a few significant points for the general process of industrialization and economic development of the country. These are discussed below.

SOCIAL SELECTIVITY

The data show that the factory system at Kota is socially selective. The factory workforce was of superior social quality as compared to the general workforce of both Kota and Rajasthan. We found that 63·4 per cent of the factory workforce were less than thirty years of age (age group 18-30 years), as compared to 27·8 per cent and 28·4 per cent of the general workforce at Kota and Rajasthan respectively that fell in the age group 15-34 years.[4] The literacy rate for

[4] *Census of India* 1961, General Economic Tables, Vol. XIV, Part II-B(i), pp. 6-37 and 88-89.

the respondents was 76·0 per cent (71·9 per cent for workers' group) against 19·05 per cent and 15·21 per cent for Kota and Rajasthan respectively. Only 55·0 per cent of respondents were of rural origin. The corresponding percentages for Kota and Rajasthan were 81·31 and 83·7 respectively. Further, only 29·0 per cent of respondents belonged to Kota, and the rest were immigrants. The average family size of the factory workforce was 5·12 as compared to 5·80 and 6·35 for the general workforce of Kota and Rajasthan respectively. Similarly, the monthly per capita family income of the respondents was Rs. 53·25 against Rs. 34·35 and Rs. 19·92 for Kota and Rajasthan respectively.

This comparison shows that compared to the general workforce of Kota and Rajasthan, the factory workforce was younger in age, more literate, better educated, less rural in their backgrounds, mostly immigrants, and had smaller size families and higher per capita income.

However, the general picture of the factory workforce does not hold good for each factory type taken separately. The majority of the workforce in 'Public B' type factories was local (80·0 per cent), relatively older in age (56·1 per cent above 30 years), urbanite (62·0 per cent), unskilled (72·0 per cent), and earned less. The 'Private A' type factory employed a workforce whose social characteristics were superior to those of its counterparts in other factory types. The only exception was 'Public A' factory wherein the workforce was more literate and skilled. It appears that enterprises with superior technology and of larger size called for better social quality in their workforce.

A notable feature was that supervisors employed in all factory types, and the workforce in 'Private A' type who had the highest earnings, also had the largest size of families. It seems that the relatively high income of these groups drew added dependents and, thus, larger families.

Cultural Inadequacy

The data also reveal that the factory system at Kota attracted a large number of persons who found their 'traditional culture inadequate'. There are several indicators of this phenomenon taking place. First, 41·4 per cent of the total factory workforce was Harijans, of whom 90·0 per cent were immigrants. They were the first group to be pushed out of the traditional culture. Second, the factories drew most of their workforce from non-farming occupations, such as non-agricultural labour and technical/mechanical groups. These persons did not own land and remained the economically marginal groups in a rural agricultural economy. Third, education has tended to disorganize the traditional culture. Most of the new entrants were literates with varying levels of education. Being socially downtrodden and economically marginal, these groups moved out in search of a new future. The acquisition of education made it possible for them to reject the traditional culture and to seek out equality of opportunity and status in a relatively achievement-oriented environment.

It is not surprising that the factories could attract local persons to a limited extent only. Agriculture and other traditional occupations are relatively more remunerative in Kota than in other areas of Rajasthan. The traditions of administrative jobs and commercial occupations are centuries old. The lower caste people were already employed in large numbers (48·0 per cent) in 'Public B' type factories. Consequently, relatively fewer persons found the traditional culture inadequate. Education tended to be a disorganizing factor in the local community as well. But, in view of the predominance of the upper castes and the tradition of white-collar occupations, the local persons sought only clerical jobs in industry.

Recruitment and Training

A factory has two choices in new recruits. It may either fill vacancies by those who possess the skills and the experience required to do specific jobs, or it may recruit men who are new to industrial occupations, and then socialize them to the industrial way and, thereby, equip them for particular tasks. The import of readily usable skills often requires building up of reward differentials in the wage hierarchy, resulting in higher costs of recruitment and a higher wage bill. On the other hand, the processes of socialization and training of new entrants to the labour-force may add to overhead costs and keep labour productivity at a low level. The management's preference for a particular alternative is influenced by the level of technology involved in the manufacturing process, the nature of the labour market, and the extent to which it is willing to assume the responsibility for the training and the socialization of its workforce.

It was mentioned earlier that factories at Kota used varying levels of technology in their production processes. The 'B' type factories required low or no skill in workers except at the supervisory level. The railway workshop ('Public A') required at least as many skilled workers as the number of machines installed. The chemical plant ('Private A') required skilled personnel on the direct process and mostly unskilled workers for ancillary jobs. The public undertakings, by definition, were more committed to assume responsibility for the training and socialization of workers than the private enterprises. Also, the industries at Kota were confronted with a seller's labour market. Under the circumstances, it was normal for the 'Private A' factories to import experience and skill for skilled jobs and also have a higher wage bill. On the other hand, the 'Public A' factory placed more emphasis on the training of operatives. 'Private B' factories attached little importance to experience except for a few key positions and were not interested in training their workforce.

We found that 68·0 per cent and 60·0 per cent of respondents in 'Public A' and 'Public B' type factories respectively had no previous job experience, as compared to 27·0 per cent and 25·0 per cent in 'Private A' and 'Private B' type factories respectively. It is obvious that the public undertakings recruited raw hands and invested in their training. This conclusion finds further support from the relatively longer employment standing of respondents employed in the public undertakings. Contrary to this, the private enterprises opted for experienced hands who were immediately usable. In particular, 'Private A' factories engaged a relatively larger number of men with previous experience of technical/mechanical jobs. It is clear that no factory employed a workforce that was drawn in any significant numbers from the farming community. Further, it was noticed that the factories at Kota provided higher earnings to their workforce than they had gained before. More workers took home a heavier pay packet than they did in their previous jobs. The income changes were substantial for the workers employed in 'Private A' factories.

Summary

To sum up the discussion, the data show that the factory workforce at Kota possessed social characteristics that were markedly superior to those possessed by the general workforce of Kota and Rajasthan. In general, the factory workforce was young, literate, and immigrant. It was heavily drawn from the lower castes and non-agricultural labour occupations. Pushed by the inadequacy of the traditional culture and attracted by the factory system, better quality men had shifted to newer occupations in search of better economic and social prospects. The data also show that education tends to disrupt the traditional culture and makes for occupational and geographic mobility of the more adventurous people. They further show that the increase in earnings is often neutralized by a corresponding increase in the dependency load on the earners. The data further reveal that the larger size enterprises with superior technology attract a workforce which is characterized by better social quality. Finally, the public undertakings have taken upon themselves a greater responsibility for training men for newer occupations. Since most of their workforce is constituted of immigrants, the advantage of this policy lies more in improving the quality of the local job market than in developing the region as such. This policy does, of course, improve the quality of labour available to the local job market, but it does nothing to improve the skills of the general population of the region.

TABLE 1

Table showing age distribution of respondents by job status

Job status	Less than 30 years	30-40 years	40 years and above
Workers	64·2	24·0	11·8
Clerks	70·6	23·5	5·8
Supervisors	48·6	24·3	27·0
Overall	63·4	24·0	12·6

TABLE 2

Table showing age distribution of respondents by factory types

Factory type	Less than 30 years	30-40 years	40 years and above
Private A	84·8	13·9	1·3
Public A	58·4	32·3	9·3
Private B	67·3	20·4	12·2
Public B	43·9	24·0	32·0
All Factories	63·4	24·0	12·6

TABLE 3

Table showing age distribution of respondents by factory types and job status

Factory type		Less than 30 years	30-40 years	40 years and above
Private A	W	85·0	15·0	0·0
	C	91·7	8·3	0·0
	S	71·4	14·3	14·3
Public A	W	60·0	30·0	10·0
	C	45·5	54·5	0·0
	S	50·0	40·0	10·0
Private B	W	68·5	20·8	10·7
	C	100·0	0·0	0·0
	S	41·6	25·0	33·4
Public B	W	44·2	26·2	29·5
	C	50·0	16·7	33·4
	S	37·5	12·5	50·0

W=Workers   S=Supervisors   C=Clerks
Unless otherwise stated, all data shown in these tables are in percentages.

TABLE 4

Table showing level of education of respondents by factory types

Factory type	Illiterate	Literate	Literates 4 to 9 years schooling	Literates High school and above
Private A	21·5	78·5	31·7	46·8
Public A	9·9	90·1	65·3	24·8
Private B	40·8	59·2	48·9	10·3
Public B	24·0	75·0	53·4	21·6
All Factories	24·0	76·0	52·4	23.6

TABLE 5

Table showing level of education of respondents by factory types and job status

Factory type		Illiterate	Literate	Literates 4 to 9 years schooling	Literates High school and above
Private A	W C S	28·3 0·0 0·0	71·7 100·0 100·0	41·7 0·0 0·0	30·0 100·0 100·0
Public A	W C S	11·4 0·0 0·0	88·6 100·0 100·0	70·0 27·2 40·0	18·6 72·8 60·0
Private B	W C S	45·4 0·0 8·3	54·6 100·0 91·7	52·4 20·0 25·0	2·2 80·0 66·7
Public B	W C S	29·5 0·0 0·0	70·5 100·0 100·0	59·0 16·7 37·5	11·5 83·3 62·5
All Factories	W C S	28·1 0·0 2·0	71·9 100·0 98·0	55·3 16·0 25·7	16·6 84·0 72·3

Table 6

Table showing classification of workers by skill in different factory types

Factory type	Unskilled	Semi-skilled	Skilled
Private A	45·0	25·0	30·0
Public A	27·0	32·0	41·0
Private B	68·0	31·0	1·0
Public B	64·0	26·0	10·0
All Factories	51·6	27·2	21·2

Table 7

Table showing the background of respondents by factory types

Factory type	Rural	Urban
Private A	72·0	28·0
Public A	56·0	44·0
Private B	64·0	36·0
Public B	38·0	62·0
All Factories	55·0	45·0

Table 8

Table showing the place of origin of respondents by factory types

Factory type	Kota	Rajasthan	Other States
Private A	33·0	27·0	40·0
Public A	9·0	36·0	55·0
Private B	24·0	36·0	40·0
Public B	80·0	12·0	8·0
All Factories	29·0	30·0	41·0

TABLE 9

Table showing caste distribution of respondents by job status

Job status	Brahmins	Kshatriyas	Vaishyas	Harijans
Workers	24·3	22·5	7·1	46·1
Clerks	28·1	25·5	23·9	22·5
Supervisors	13·8	41·4	37·9	6·9
Overall	23·8	24·1	10·6	41·4

TABLE 10

Table showing caste distribution of respondents by factory types

Factory type	Brahmins	Kshatriyas	Vaishyas	Harijans
Private A	33·8	19·7	15·5	31·0
Public A	31·8	27·3	9·1	31·8
Private B	13·4	21·0	10·9	54·6
Public B	15·6	28·1	7·8	48·4
All Factories	23·8	24·1	10·6	41·4

TABLE 11

Table showing the family size of respondents by factory types and job status

Factory type	Workers	Clerks	Supervisors	Overall
Private A	4·98	5·58	8·14	6·23
Public A	5·10	5·09	6·29	5·46
Private B	4·73	2·60	5·16	4·16
Public B	4·78	5·50	3·62	4·63
All Factories	4·90	4·69	5·78	5·12

TABLE 12

Table showing economic status of the members of respondents' families by factory types and job status

Factory type	Workers D	Workers E	Clerks D	Clerks E	Supervisors D	Supervisors E	Overall D	Overall E
Private A	3·40	1·58	3·75	1·83	6·28	1·85	4·17	1·75
Public A	3·82	1·30	3·72	1·36	4·90	1·30	4·14	1·32
Private B	3·29	1·43	1·40	1·20	3·50	1·66	3·01	1·43
Public B	3·32	1·45	3·33	2·16	2·50	1·12	4·30	1·48
All Factories	3·46	1·44	3·05	1·64	4·30	1·48	3·61	1·52

D=Dependents E=Earners

TABLE 13

Table showing monthly family income and per capita income of respondents by factory types

Factory type	Workers Monthly (Rs.)	Workers Per Capita (Rs.)	Clerks Monthly (Rs.)	Clerks Per Capita (Rs.)	Supervisors Monthly (Rs.)	Supervisors Per Capita (Rs.)
Private A	179·10	35·96	254·16	45·55	819·43	100·67
Public A	146·13	28·65	217·72	42·77	418·90	67·56
Private B	127·94	27·05	152·40	58·61	320·58	62·13
Public B	126·00	26·36	252·33	45·88	250·12	69·09
All Factories	144·79	29·51	219·15	48·20	452·26	74·86

Average monthly family income of respondents= Rs. 272·66
Monthly per capita income of respondents= Rs. 53·25

TABLE 14

Table showing distribution of workers by their 'take-home' pay and factory types

Factory type	Workers earning less than Rs. 100 p.m.	Workers earning Rs. 100-200 p.m.	Workers earning more than Rs. 200 p.m.
Private A	32·9	49·3	17·8
Public A	37·3	59·0	3·7
Private B	65·3	30·6	4·1
Public B	54·3	38·7	6·6

TABLE 15

Table showing distribution of workers by their gross salary and migratory status

Income	Private A Local	Private A Outsider	Public A Local	Public A Outsider	Private B Local	Private B Outsider	Public B Local	Public B Outsider
Less than Rs. 100 p.m.	55	35	67	32	97	50	63	40
Rs. 100-200 p.m.	45	44	33	67	—	46	37	60
Rs. 200 and above p.m.	—	21	—	1	3	4	—	—

TABLE 16

Table showing level of income and level of education of local workers

Income	High school and above Private A	High school and above Public B	4 to 9 years schooling Private A	4 to 9 years schooling Public B	Illiterate Private A	Illiterate Public B
Less than Rs. 100 p.m.	67	67	44	100	60	100
Rs. 100-200 p.m.	33	33	56	—	40	—
Rs. 200 and above p.m.	0	—	0	—	0	0

TABLE 17

Table showing respondents by number of previous employers by factory types

Previous employer	Private A	Public A	Private B	Public B	All factories
0	27	68	25	60	46
1	47	21	46	23	34
2	17	6	14	8	11
3	6	2	15	9	8
4 and above	3	3	—	—	1

TABLE 18

Table showing previous jobs held by respondents by occupation and by factory types

Type of previous employment	Private A	Public A	Private B	Public B	All factories
Farming	5	11	10	11	9
Non-agricultural labour	25	42	42	30	37
Artisan/Craftsman	7	5	5	2	5
Technical/Mechanical	43	18	29	34	30
Civil Service	14	12	5	17	10
Trade and Commerce	1	1	2	2	2
Miscellaneous	5	11	7	4	7

TABLE 19

Table showing respondents by occupation, previous jobs held and their fathers' occupations

Type of previous employment	Private A Self	Private A Father	Public A Self	Public A Father	Private B Self	Private B Father	Public B Self	Public B Father	All factories Self	All factories Father
Farming	5	48	11	44	10	52	11	28	9	42
Non-agricultural labour	25	2	42	5	42	5	30	7	37	5
Artisan/Craftsman	7	12	5	5	5	11	2	7	5	9
Technical/Mechanical	43	2	18	1	29	5	34	7	30	4
Civil Service	14	23	12	29	5	6	17	41	10	25
Trade and Commerce	1	5	1	9	2	9	2	8	2	8
Miscellaneous	5	8	11	7	7	12	4	2	7	7

TABLE 20

Table showing the location of previous jobs of respondents by factory types

Location	Private A	Public A	Private B	Public B	All factories
Kota	9·2	8·3	11·9	—	9·2
Native State	51·6	39·3	61·6	88·6	58·6
Places other than the above	39·2	52·4	26·5	11·4	32·2

TABLE 21

Table showing workers who held jobs previously by their highest monthly 'take-home' pay in any previous job

Monthly 'take-home' pay	Private A	Public A	Private B	Public B	All factories
Less than Rs. 100	58	68	85	59	68
Rs. 100-200	42	32	15	41	32
Rs. 200 and above	0	0	0	0	0

TABLE 22

Table showing respondents by their 'take-home' pay from the current job (CJ) and the highest ever 'take-home' pay from a previous job (PJ)

Monthly 'take-home' pay	Private A CJ	Private A PJ	Public A CJ	Public A PJ	Private B CJ	Private B PJ	Public B CJ	Public B PJ	All factories CJ	All factories PJ
Less than Rs. 100	33	58	37	68	65	85	54	59	48	68
Rs. 100-200	49	42	59	32	31	15	39	41	44	32
Rs. 200 and above	18	0	4	0	4	0	7	0	8	0

TABLE 23

Table showing the reasons for which respondents changed previous jobs

Reason	Private A	Public A	Private B	Public B	All factories
Health	3·4	1·2	5·5	15·1	5·4
Family	11·5	7·1	7·0	3·8	7·5
Far away from native place	1·1	—	1·0	—	0·7
Conflict with supervisors	2·2	2·4	7·0	1·9	4·5
Closure of employing agency	6·0	—	6·5	—	4·5
Terminated	14·9	25·0	17·9	28·3	20·0
For higher wages	56·6	46·4	38·6	49·1	45·2
Miscellaneous	—	9·6	8·0	1·8	5·8
No reason	3·4	8·3	8·5	—	

TABLE 24

Table showing distribution of respondents by duration of unemployment spells

Period of unemployment	Private A	Public A	Private B	Public B	All factories
None	81·8	20·0	46·7	42·8	42·4
Less than 1 year	—	36·0	26·7	28·6	26·0
1-2 years	18·2	20·0	10·0	—	13·7
2-3 years	—	12·0	6·6	28·6	9·6
3-4 years	—	12·0	10·0	—	8·3

TABLE 25

Table showing respondents according to each place of residence during unemployment by factory types

Place	Private A	Public A	Private B	Public B	All factories
Stayed on	64	64	64	57	63
Returned to native place	36	28	29	43	31
Migrated to other places	—	8	7	—	6

TABLE 26

Table showing respondents according to sources of livelihood during unemployment by factory types

Source of livelihood	Private A	Public A	Private B	Public B	All factories
Dependence on friends/relatives	54	88	39	71	62
Borrowing from others	—	—	3	29	8
Past savings	28	—	6	—	9
Casual work	18	12	52	—	21

Chapter IV

IN THE JOB MARKET

Introduction

The social characteristics and the employment experience of the factory workforce have been discussed in the preceding chapter. This chapter concerns itself with the changes in the employees' perceptions of the job market at Kota. The analysis is based on the qualitative responses of the respondents on the questions asked of them. This will enable us to comment on the extent to which the exposure to factory employment changed employees' perceptions, and oriented them to become a stable industrial workforce.

The experiences of the employees of their current employment were varied and complex. The generalizations made on the basis of the data presented at the end of this chapter are subject to two limitations. First, employees' perception of the Kota job market may not necessarily be the result of their employment experience at Kota. The previous job experience could have equally conditioned their responses about the current employment. Forty-six per cent of respondents had, however, no previous job experience (Chapter II), and their responses could certainly be considered to reflect the impact of employment at Kota. Second, respondents varied in the length of service in their current employment. Though 44·0 per cent of the respondents had lengths of service of five or more years, they showed considerable variation by factory types and job status. Sixty-eight and fifty-one per cent of respondents of 'Private A' and 'Private B' respectively had up to two years' service against 6·0 and 4·0 per cent in 'Public A' and 'Public B'. In the latter type factories, 81·0 per cent and 77·0 per cent of respondents respectively had five or more years of service against 3·0 and 9·0 per cent in this category in the former types (Table 1). Job status-wise,

45·0 per cent of workers, 32·0 per cent of clerks, and 43·0 per cent of supervisors had five or more years' length of service (Table 2). The differences in the length of service by job status are not so marked as those by factory types; nonetheless, they are significant. However, despite these two limitations, the data yield meaningful generalizations.

Perception of Job Market

The employees' perception of the Kota job market brought out two significant points. They perceived a high employment potential in the Kota job market, and also found that the job market required them to possess skill, education, and training of a higher level.

The respondents' perception of the employment potential at Kota was contrary to the common belief that there was acute unemployment in the country, and that jobs were difficult to be found. The respondents were asked the question, 'If you happen to lose your current job, how much time are you likely to take to find another job at Kota?' Only 23·0 per cent of respondents were uncertain of the time, 11·0 per cent expected to take less than a month, 52·0 per cent between one and six months, and 14·0 per cent up to one year (Table 9). The comparison by factory types revealed a superior perception of employment potential of respondents working in 'Private A', where 20·0 per cent of them expected to find alternative jobs within one month, and only 17·0 per cent were uncertain of future prospects. About half of the respondents in each factory type stated that it might take them up to six months to find alternative jobs at Kota. Analyzed by job status (Table 10), clerks perceived a better employment potential at Kota than the other two groups. While 23·0 per cent of clerks expected to find alternative jobs at Kota within one month, only 9·0 per cent of workers and 11·0 per cent of supervisors felt similarly. Again, only 13·0 per cent of clerks were uncertain of the time it would take them to find an alternative job at Kota against 24·0 per cent of workers, and 28·0 per cent of supervisors in this category. Thus, the members of the factory workforce were confident that they could find alternative jobs at Kota within a reasonable period of time.

The respondents were also aware of the demands of the job market on them, and the manner in which a job could be secured. Forty-nine per cent of respondents stated that future jobs would require them to possess good education and training (Table 5), and 76·0 per cent felt that higher education would help them in improving their employment opportunities (Table 7). Sixty-two per cent of respondents stated that demonstrated merit counted most in getting a job at Kota (Table 5). They were also of the opinion that the Kota job market offered a structured mechanism for entry. Sixty-two per cent of respondents held that formal inquiries with companies, employment exchanges, and newspaper advertisements were the best methods of finding information about vacancies at Kota.

The respondents thus perceived a job market at Kota that was both favourable and structured. They thought it demanded skill, education and training, and that it recognized merit. The job market was viewed as operating through formally structured mechanisms, wherein particularistic attributes of individuals were less important. The respondents dismissed the fear of unemployment. They perceived high employment potential in the Kota job market, and regarded themselves as capable of availing of it.

Changes in Perceptions

In order to find out the changes in their perceptions of the job market as well as what it required of them, the respondents were asked questions on their reasons for taking up their current factory job, sources of vacancy information, how in fact they secured jobs, and the time that it took. They were further asked to respond to the same questions in the context of a future job, if they were obliged to find one. The responses concerning the two points of time were compared and changes, if any, noted. Similarly, the respondents were asked to state the level of education and income that they would like to achieve, and also the occupations they desired most. The levels of income,

On Selecting Factory Jobs

The respondents were asked to state the reasons for selecting their current jobs. The responses (Table 3) show that 58·0 per cent of respondents had no choice in selecting their current jobs. They picked up whatever jobs first came their way. The incidence of the limited choice in selecting the job varied by factory types. Only 37·0 per cent of respondents in 'Private A' reported lack of freedom in the choice of their current jobs against 67·0 per cent in 'Private B', 63·0 per cent in 'Public A', and 60·0 per cent in 'Public B'. Those who took up factory jobs because 'it was better than any other type of work' accounted for 26·0 per cent in 'Private A', and varied from 10·0 to 16·0 per cent in other factory types. Another 21·0 and 30·0 per cent of respondents in 'Private A' and 'Public B' respectively took up factory jobs because they were 'qualified/trained for such work'. The respondents under this category numbered 9·0 and 6·0 per cent in 'Public A' and 'Private B' respectively. Relatively few respondents gave 'regular higher earnings' as a consideration in their selection of their current jobs.

On the whole, the process by which current jobs were selected was characterized by 'no choice' or 'lack of freedom' in respect of the majority of respondents. Amongst those who could exercise a choice, the majority took to factory work as they regarded it as qualitatively better than other types of work. A slightly lesser number chose factory jobs because of their specialized qualifications and training, and still fewer because of the higher regular earnings. The respondents employed in 'Private A' stood out as a distinct group insofar as the process of job selection was concerned. Sixty-three per cent of respondents in this factory exercised a conscious choice in favour of the factory job.

Most of the respondents desired to continue to work in factories if they were to lose their current jobs. Table 4 shows that only 14·0 per cent of respondents were unwilling to take up factory work in future, 25·0 per cent were unsure, and 61·0 per cent were certain that they wanted to continue to work in factories. An inter-factory type comparison showed that employees in 'B' type factories were less keen on factory jobs than those in 'A' type.

It is obvious from the above analysis that factory work experience brought a basic change in the perceptions and attitudes of the respondents towards factory work. Though 58·0 per cent of respondents had taken to factory work by chance, at the time of the survey 61·0 per cent had decided to continue in it. This attitudinal change in favour of factory work was the highest in the case of 'Public A' and the lowest in 'Private A' as shown below.

Factory type	Percentage that held current jobs by choice	Percentage that want factory jobs in future
Private A	63	67
Public A	37	65
Private B	34	55
Public B	40	51

The high degree of change in the attitudes of the workforce employed in 'Public A' might be due to their greater length of service. It might also be due to a lesser desire to move from a known to an unknown vocation at a relatively older age. But the employees might not have given such a favourable response if, on balance, their work experience was not a happy one. We noted in Chapter II that 'Public A' undertook considerable responsibility in training the workforce, and provided higher job security and the highest fringe benefits and welfare services in the area. All these measures might have contributed to the attitudinal changes. The majority of the workforce employed in 'Private A' were already motivated to factory work. As such, there was only a little scope for further attitudinal change in their case.

Entering the Job Market

The respondents' entry into the job market was studied by asking them, 'What were the sources of vacancy information, what mattered most in getting the current job, and how much time did it take to get the job?' They were then asked, 'What would matter most in getting a future job, what would be the sources of vacancy information and how much time would it take?' The responses on these and other related questions were compared and the results presented in Tables 5, 8, 9, and 10.

Vacancy Information

Table 8 presents the respondents' sources of vacancy information for their current jobs and the perceived sources for future jobs. It was found that 70·0 per cent of respondents came to know of the current employment opportunities from either friends or relatives. Another 13·0 per cent learnt of vacancies from jobbers, mistris, and employers' recruiting agents. The formal sources of vacancy information, such as newspaper advertisements and employment exchanges, played an insignificant role in the process of securing the current jobs. A comparison of the responses by factory types did not bring out any differences except that employment exchanges were made use of by 29·0 per cent of respondents in 'Private A'.

Employees' perception of usable sources of vacancy information underwent a material change insofar as future jobs were concerned. It can be observed from Table 8 that 46·0 per cent of respondents would like to make direct inquiries of the prospective employer. The informal vacancy informants—friends, relatives, and employers' agents —were not seen as useful any longer. Only 23.0 per cent of respondents thought of these sources in the context of future jobs. Newspaper advertisements were seen as relatively more useful.

A particular reference needs to be made to employment exchanges. It is a statutory obligation on the part of employers to notify all vacancies to the employment exchange in the area and to consider for appointment the candidates sponsored by the latter. However, most of the respondents did not make much use of this service nor did they perceive it to be of any importance in getting jobs.

Getting a Job

Employees' perception of 'what mattered most in getting the current and future jobs' are presented in Table 5. It was found that 'contact with those who matter in the company' helped 40·0 per cent of respondents in getting their current jobs. Another 21·0 per cent of respondents secured jobs through social contacts. Only 37·0 per cent of respondents reported that they had secured their current positions primarily due to their qualifications, such as education, training, and work experience.

The experience of the job market brought about an important change in the employees' perception of the role of 'pulls and connections'. Only 28·0 per cent of respondents thought that connections with 'key' persons in companies could help them in securing future jobs. Social contacts were no longer considered significant in getting jobs. Sixty-two per cent of respondents concluded that education, training and work experience would matter most in securing jobs in the future.

Thus, though the majority of the respondents reported that they secured their current jobs with the help of 'pulls and connections', they did not think that such props would pay dividends in getting jobs in the future. They thought that companies looked for efficient hands and that those who possessed necessary skill and experience would be able to get jobs in the future without any extraneous help.

Time Required

Tables 9 and 10 show the time taken by the respondents to secure their current jobs, and the expected time in getting future jobs. It will be noticed that 49·0 per cent of respondents took one to six months in getting their current jobs, and that 39·0 per cent took up to one year. It was found that no one in the public sector could get his job within a month of his looking for one. This might have been due to the lengthy selection procedures prevalent there. But 18·0 per cent of respondents in 'Private A' and 6·0 per cent in 'Private B' got their current jobs within a month. Subject to minor variations, the position was not very different in regard to the time required to find the future job. More than half of the respondents still thought that they would require one to six months to find alternative jobs. Those who expected to find the future job within a month accounted for 11·0 per cent, which was double of those who got their current jobs within the same period.

A major change took place in the group from '6 months to a year'. Against 39·0 per cent of respondents who took that long to find their current jobs, only 14·0 per cent expected to take that much time in finding jobs in the future. The change was due to a shift in the perception of employees in the public sector and in 'Private B' type factories. Analyzed by job status (Table 10), we could find no change in the 'one to six months' group. However, major changes occurred in the workers' and clerks' groups. More clerks (23·0 per cent) thought that they could find their future jobs in less than a month's time. Also, against 31·0 per cent of workers who took six months to one year to find their current jobs, only 14·0 per cent felt that it would take them that long to find jobs in the future.

On the whole, about half the respondents took one to six months to find the current jobs, and they felt that the position would not be much different insofar as future jobs were concerned. However, a much smaller percentage (14·0) expected to take longer than six months to find jobs in the future. This not only indicated the perception of a better employment potential in the job market, but also suggested a workforce at once more committed and more familiar with selection procedures which themselves had been improved in the interval.

EDUCATION AND TRAINING

In view of the importance given by the respondents to education and training, they were asked about their educational aspirations: 'If it were possible, how much education would you like to have?' The replies are presented in Table 6. Only 5·0 per cent of respondents were unsure about the level of education to which they aspired; another 3·0 per cent wanted no further education. Of the rest, 25·0 per cent wanted to study up to high school, 27·0 per cent up to B.A., 13·0 per cent up to M.A., and the remaining 26·0 per cent wished to acquire professional training. The majority in the workers' group wanted to qualify to the high school certificate standard. Most of the clerks desired Bachelor's or Master's degree, and most of the supervisors wanted further professional training.

Fourteen of the 17 per cent of workers that were matriculates wanted to study up to B.A. and qualify themselves for clerical jobs. Similarly, 53·0 out of the 83·0 per cent non-matriculate workers wanted to complete high school, another 19·0 per cent B.A., and only 4·0 per cent expressed a desire for technical training. The desire for technical education was also little evident among the clerks. Out of 84·0 per cent of clerks who were matriculates, 57·0 per cent were keen to take their B.A. or M.A. degrees and qualify themselves for higher white-collar jobs, and the rest desired technical education. The quest for technical education was the highest amongst the supervisors' group. Sixty-six per cent out of 74 per cent matriculate supervisors wanted either technical or scientific education. Only half of the non-matriculate supervisors wanted further technical education. It will be noticed from Table 7 that 76·0 per cent of the respondents who desired to improve their educational qualifications wanted to do so only to improve their employment conditions. Only 19·0 per cent of respondents, all of whom were workers, wanted higher education to enable them to change from their current occupation to office work.

On the whole, the respondents evinced a keen desire to acquire higher education. The majority of both the clerks and workers preferred general education to technical education. Most of the respondents—nearly two-thirds of them in 'B' type factories and about one-half in 'Private A'—did not desire further training. It was only in

'Public A' that 84·0 per cent of workers were in favour of training.

In general, respondents seemed anxious for general education but were apathetic to training ('Public A' being an exception). Such an attitude might be due to one or more reasons. It might be that employees considered high school level education as the base that should be achieved before training became relevant to promotion or improving employment conditions. Apathy to training might also be traced to the absence of promotions earned by most of them. Eighty-six per cent of respondents in the private sector and 51·0 per cent in 'Public B' had earned no promotions at all. Superior 'jobs' were occupied by persons who had higher education. This provided evidence that higher education paid more dividends than better skills. This logic found support from 'Public A' (which provided training) where a greater desire for training was associated with a higher rate of promotion.

Conclusions

The foregoing discussion shows that most of the respondents took up factory jobs at Kota not from any particular choice. They learnt of the employment opportunities at Kota mostly through friends and relatives. 'Pulls', 'connections', and recommendations helped most of the respondents in securing their current jobs. And it generally took them up to six months to secure employment.

The exposure to industrial employment at Kota enabled most of the respondents to make a more objective assessment of the local job market and its operations. It also influenced their perception of and attitude towards factory jobs and gave them a greater confidence in their ability to stay in factory employment. At the time of the investigation, most of the respondents perceived that the Kota job market had considerable employment potential. They were also in a position to identify the formal mechanisms that existed for securing a job. Direct inquiries with the companies and newspaper advertisements, by and large, took the place of friends and relatives as sources of vacancy information. Merit in terms of job qualifications and proficiency in work took the place of good connections as levers for getting a job. More important, most of the respondents felt that they possessed the ability to secure a job in the future without any external help. They knew what they should possess, and also how to go about getting a job. Most of them felt confident that if they wanted to find a new job, they could get it within six months. They neither perceived nor feared unemployment. Most of them were conscious that they should improve their educational level and acquire better skills on the current job.

The discussions brought out a few points that would help to explain changes in the respondents' perception of the job market. Generally high school level of education was considered by all as the basic qualification for securing any worthwhile job. Currently, only 24·0 per cent of the respondents were educated up to high school and the rest desired that level. Most companies preferred high school education for any skilled, clerical, or supervisory position. Only employees in this category earned promotions. Second, the attitude towards technical training was more favourable when it was accompanied by opportunities for promotion. It was only in 'Public A' that respondents overwhelmingly sought training. This was also the factory which offered training and in which 86·0 per cent of respondents did earn promotions over the years. Third, though the respondents were more favourably inclined towards factory work, the maximum change occurred in the case of 'Public A' only. The attitudinal changes in favour of factory work took place faster when they were accompanied by job security, fringe benefits, housing, and welfare services.

The changes in perceptions, attitudes, values, and ethos of the workforce are significant from the point of view of employers. They indicate the need for greater emphasis on the formal channels and methods of recruitment. The favourable attitudes of employees to achievement, and variables such as education, training, and performance provide the necessary basis for improving human efficiency and organizational effectiveness. It may be stated that, on the whole, the factory system at Kota initiated changes in the attitudes and values of its workforce and helped them to a greater acceptance of the industrial way of life. The analysis also shows that once the process of industrialization has been started, the necessary ethos will emerge along with it. This phenomenon, in turn, will facilitate workers' adjustment to the factory system.

TABLE 1

Table showing distribution of respondents by length of service in their present employment

Length of service	Private A	Public A	Private B	Public B	All factories
Less than 1 year	33	4	33	3	18
1-2 years	35	2	18	1	13
2-3 years	28	3	25	8	15
3-4 years	1	4	12	8	7
4-5 years	—	6	3	3	4
5 years and above	3	81	9	77	44

TABLE 2

Table showing respondents' length of service in the present employment by job status

Length of service	Workers	Clerks	Supervisors
Less than 1 year	18	24	14
1-2 years	12	21	16
2-3 years	15	15	22
3-4 years	7	6	3
4-5 years	3	3	3
5 years and more	45	32	43

In these tables the figures are in percentages.

TABLE 3

Table showing respondents' reasons for selecting the current job in the factory

Reason	Private A	Public A	Private B	Public B	All factories
Qualified/trained	21	9	6	30	14
Higher or regular earning	16	12	12	0	11
Factory work better than other work	26	16	16	10	17
No choice	37	63	67	60	58

TABLE 4

Table showing responses about respondents' search for future jobs if the current job is lost

Type	Yes	No	Not sure
Private A	67	10	23
Public A	65	14	21
Private B	55	17	28
Public B	51	13	36
All factories	61	14	25

TABLE 5

Table showing the distribution of respondents on 'what mattered most in getting a job'

Things that matter	Current job	Future job
1. Contact with those who matter in the company	40	28
2. Education & training	23	49
3. Work experience	14	13
4. Social contacts	21	5
5. Cannot say	2	5

(Percentage of responses)

Table 6

Table showing the distribution of respondents by the desired level of education by job status

Level of education	Workers	Clerks	Supervisors	All factories
Up to High School	53	8	13	25
Up to B.A.	23	35	24	27
Post-Graduate	7	27	6	13
Professional degree/Diploma	4	27	49	26
No improvement	3	—	5	3
Not sure	9	3	3	5

EDUCATION

Workers :

    Out of 17% matriculates
            14% want higher education
            3% not sure

    Out of 83% non-matriculates
            53% want to do matric
            19% want to do B.A./Higher education
            4% want to have training
            6% not sure

Clerks :

    Out of 16% non-matriculates
            8% want to do high school
            5% want further education
            3% not sure

    Out of 84% matriculates
            35% want to do B.A.
            22% want to do M.A.
            27% want professional training

Supervisors :

    2% illiterates—want to do nothing

    Out of 26% non-matriculates
            13% want to do matric
            13% want to have technical training

    Out of 74% matriculates
            36% want technical training
            30% want to do B.Sc./M.Sc.
            5% want to do nothing
            3% not sure

TABLE 7

Table showing respondents by the purpose for which education is desired

Purpose	Percentage
For improving employment conditions	76
To change to office job	19
For increasing knowledge	3
Uncertain	2

TABLE 8

Table showing respondents by sources of vacancy information for the current job (CJ) and perceived sources for the future job (FJ)

Source	Private A CJ	Private A FJ	Public A CJ	Public A FJ	Private B CJ	Private B FJ	Public B CJ	Public B FJ	All factories CJ	All factories FJ
Relatives & friends	60	3	84	30	65	21	86	20	70	21
Jobbers/mistris/ employer's agents	2	0	9	1	22	3	9	1	13	2
Direct enquiry at the gate	7	47	0	36	11	55	0	49	5	46
Employment exchanges	29	16	3	5	2	2	2	1	2	5
Newspaper advertisement	2	29	4	23	0	16	3	25	10	22
No answer	0	5	0	5	0	3	0	4	0	4

TABLE 9

Table showing respondents by time taken to secure the current job and perception of time required to secure a job in the future

Time taken	Private A CJ	Private A FJ	Public A CJ	Public A FJ	Private B CJ	Private B FJ	Public B CJ	Public B FJ	All factories CJ	All factories FJ
Less than one month	18	20	0	2	6	12	0	9	5	11
1-6 months	62	55	32	48	52	52	48	52	49	52
6 months to a year	14	8	60	15	35	15	44	18	39	14
Not sure	6	17	8	35	7	21	8	21	7	23

TABLE 10

Table showing respondents by time taken to secure the current job and the perception of time required to secure a job in the future by job status

Time taken	Workers CJ	Workers FJ	Clerks CJ	Clerks FJ	Supervisors CJ	Supervisors FJ	All factories CJ	All factories FJ
Less than one month	1	9	9	23	6	11	5	11
1-6 months	57	52	64	54	65	44	49	52
6 months to a year	31	15	23	10	24	17	39	14
Not sure	11	24	4	13	5	28	7	23

TABLE 11

Table showing the distribution of respondents on 'the required basis for promotions'

Basis for promotion	Private A	Public A	Private B	Public B	All factories
Established seniority	2	13	3	9	7
Demonstrated merit	77	56	62	60	64
Suitability	7	16	7	10	10
Ability to be on the right side of the boss	10	14	14	17	14
No reply	4	1	14	4	6

TABLE 12

Table showing number of promotions earned by employees in their present employment by factory types

No. of promotions	Private A	Public A	Private B	Public B	All factories
No promotion	86	14	86	51	55
One	14	39	14	28	25
Two	—	36	1	16	15
Three	—	9	—	3	4
Four	—	2	—	2	1

Chapter V

ADJUSTMENT TO WORK

Introduction

THE central concern of this chapter is to focus attention on the employees' adjustment to work.[1] More specifically, we are interested to know the extent of the respondents' adjustment to work and the manner in which it varied by factory types and job status. How was employees' adjustment to work affected by the nature of the technology, the size and ownership of enterprises they worked for, and by their own status in the group? What were the important socio-personal attributes of workers that influenced their adjustment to work?

The Measure

A measure of the employees' 'adjustment to work' can be developed by utilizing either the organizational data or the individual responses. The measure of adjustment to work based on organizational data may take into account employees' efficiency and output, rates of absenteeism and labour turnover, extent of disciplinary action against them, functioning of suggestion schemes and joint committees, etc. The employee-oriented measure will be based on the employees' expectations from and perceptions of several of their job aspects as well as their attitudes towards a job. The present analysis utilizes the employee-oriented measure. The choice of the measure was dictated by two considerations. First, the data that were necessary for developing an organization-oriented measure were not available in all the factories studied. Many factories did not have a proper system of record keeping, which rendered even

[1] The concept of 'adjustment to work' has been discussed in Chapter I.

the available data generally less usable. Second, our own interests and competency lay in the area of attitude measurements. Therefore, we set out to determine workers' adjustment to work by measuring their attitudes towards work.

The Job Attitude Scale (JAS)

The job attitude scale was developed out of Part B of the questionnaire given as Appendix-A. Questions 1 to 22 constituted the scale, and they were used for the purpose. The questions related to such areas of work as wages, job security, opportunities for advancement, housing, supervision, work group, and working conditions. Each question required a respondent to express himself on that particular item in one of the three given response categories, separated by approximately equal intervals from the point of view of the degree of feeling. Each response was assigned a numerical value that ranged from 0 to 2. The total score on all the questions was taken to represent the overall level of a respondent's adjustment to work. The possible range of score on these 22 items was from 0 to 44. Those respondents who obtained one sigma below the Mean Work Adjustment Score were considered to have lower adjustment, and those with one sigma above the Mean as having higher adjustment. The high scoring and the low scoring groups were compared by means of the Chi Square Test[2] on each item. The modification thus made resulted in an acceptable level of internal consistency and homogeneity. The external validity of the scale was determined by correlating its total score to the score of a five-point rating scale covering almost the same areas of work.[3] The Pearson's Product Moment (r) obtained was 0.62. The split half reliability of the scale by the Spearman-Brown Formula

---

[2] For the purposes of this test 3x2 tables were planned to be used. But it was soon found that many of the cells of these tables had frequencies of less than five in the middle category making it necessary to combine frequencies in this category with other categories in due proportions. Therefore 2x2 tables were used for the Chi Square. The advantage of this method was that, with df=1, this test became sensitive to the direction of results.

[3] See items No. 1 to 7, Part B of the questionnaire given as Appendix-A.

was 0·79. Thus, the JAS proved to be a satisfactory measure of employee adjustment to work.

The procedure for developing the JAS required several stages of work. A pilot study involving 130 interviews resulted in modifications in some of the draft questionnaire items. The homogeneity and the internal consistency of the questionnaire were worked out through an item analysis in which the uppermost 27·0 per cent of the protocol were compared with the lowest 27·0 per cent. The scale thus developed was administered to the respondents and scored with the help of a specially prepared key. The total Mean Score for all the respondents as well as for each of the twelve groups was computed. In order to determine the critical values[4] for the significance of difference between the Means of different groups, standard deviations of the group Means and of the total Mean were worked out. The data thus processed are presented at the relevant places in the discussion, as are also the tables at the end of the chapter.

The Results

Adjustment to Work by Factory Types

The Overall Mean Score obtained for the sample was 26·28 (S.D.=8·37). The results of other studies of similar groups of Indian respondents were not available to us; hence, we were unable to know the relative extent of adjustment to work of our respondents. Therefore, we attempted an intra-group comparison of adjustment to work of sub-groups by factory types and job status of respondents.

An examination of Table 1 shows that the Mean Scale Scores vary in a descending order by factory types. The Mean Scale Score for 'Private A' was 29·78, followed by

---

[4]Critical ratios were determined on the null hypothesis that on the given scale there were no real differences in the Means of all the four factory types. The null hypothesis was rejected and the differences described as statistically significant when it was found that the critical value obtained was likely to occur by chance five or fewer times in 100 if the true difference between one or any other Means was really zero. In such a case, it was assumed that the obtained difference was not due to chance alone.

All discussions in this chapter present results which are statistically significant at the five per cent level of confidence.

TABLE 1

Table showing mean job attitude scores and standard deviations by factory types and job status of respondents

Job status		Factory types				Nature of enterprises		Size of factories		Total of all factories
		Private A	Public A	Private B	Public B	Private sector	Public sector	A type	B type	
(1)		(2)	(3)	(4)	(5)	(6)	(7)	(8)	(9)	(10)
Workers	Means	28·90	25·75	25·08	23·49	28·28	23·08	26·1	24·57	25·63
	S.Ds	7·8	7·5	8·9	7·92	8·75	7·7	7·7	8·63	8·25
Clerks	Means	30·0	24·91	27·80	23·00	29·35	24·24	27·57	26·1	26·79
	S.Ds	7·42	6·38	9·17	8·76	8·01	7·41	7·5	9·3	8·13
Supervisors	Means	37·11	27·00	33·25	34·88	34·67	30·5	31·11	33·9	32·66
	S.Ds	2·80	7·27	7·61	2·69	6·55	6·89	7·2	6·8	7·03
Total Employees	Means	29·78	27·01	25·44	24·67	27·22	25·88	27·02	25·4	26·28
	S.Ds	7·61	7·54	9·11	8·33	8·86	7·78	7·7	8·8	8·37

Overall mean score 26·28

27·01 for 'Public A', by 25·44 for 'Private B', and by 24·67 for 'Public B' factories. Six inter-factory type comparisons of the observed differences among the Mean Scores of the four types revealed that except in the case of 'Private B' and 'Public B', all other differences were statistically significant. The results also indicated that the respondents in 'Private A' factory displayed higher adjustment to work as compared to those in all other factory types. Whereas respondents in 'Public A' displayed a slightly higher level of adjustment, those in 'Private B' and 'Public B' revealed a relatively lower level of adjustment.

By Institutional Factors

OWNERSHIP

The adjustment to work of the respondents in the private enterprises was compared with that of those in the public undertakings. The Mean Score of all the respondents in the private enterprises was 27·22 as against 25·88 for those in the public undertakings. But the Mean difference is not statistically significant (CR=1·81). However, the difference between the Means of 'Private A' and 'Public A' does attain the acceptable level of significance. This shows that ownership had significance to the employees' adjustment to work only in bigger size plants which also utilized superior technology. Respondents employed in the smaller size private enterprises tended to score higher on the scale than their counterparts in the smaller size public undertakings. However, the differences were not significant.

SIZE

A perusal of the Mean Scores by the size of factories in columns 8 and 9 of Table 1 reveals that the respondents in 'A' type factories had significantly higher scores (Mean 27·02) in comparison to those in 'B' type factories (Mean 25·4). This shows that the respondents employed in the bigger size factories which also used superior technology ('A' type) had superior adjustment to work as compared to those working in the smaller size factories using simple technology ('B' type).

JOB STATUS

Column 10 of Table 1 shows the differences in the adjustment to work of respondents by their job status. The Mean Scores for workers, clerks, and supervisors was 25·63, 26·79, and 32·66 respectively. The supervisors showed the highest level of adjustment to work followed in order by the clerks and the workers. The differences in the Mean Scores of the clerks and the workers were not statistically significant. Therefore, the higher Mean Scores of the clerks' group could not be considered as significantly different from those of the workers' group. A further examination of Table 1 brings out that in all the factory types except 'Public A', supervisors displayed a level of adjustment that was much higher than those of the clerks and the workers. In 'Public A', the Mean Scores of all the three groups were more or less equal. Thus, although the worker-clerk *versus* the supervisor differences of Mean Scores were of general tendency, the extent of differences varied considerably—1·25 in 'Public A', 8·17 in 'Private B', 8·21 in 'Private B', and 11·39 in 'Public B' type factories.

The ranking of the Means of the twelve job status groups is given in Table 2 in the order of their superiority of adjustment to work.

It may be noticed from Table 2 that the workers' group in 'Private A' obtained a higher score than the clerks' and the supervisors' groups in 'Public A'. The analysis shows that, though the higher job status of an employee tended to contribute towards superior adjustment to work, it could only be one of the many of its other determinants.

To sum up the foregoing findings, we found that the extent of adjustment to work was the highest in 'Private A', followed in the order by 'Public A', 'Private B', and 'Public B'. The respondents in bigger size factories using superior technology displayed superior adjustment to work than those working in the smaller size factories using simple technology. Such differences were significant in the case of

TABLE 2

Table showing the ranking of the means of twelve job status groups

Status of respondents	Factory type	Mean	Rank
Supervisor	Private A	37·11	1
Supervisor	Public B	34·88	2
Supervisor	Private B	33·25	3
Clerk	Private A	30·00	4
Worker	Private A	28·90	5
Clerk	Private B	27·80	6
Supervisor	Public A	27·00	7
Worker	Public A	25·75	8
Worker	Private B	25·08	9
Clerk	Public A	24·91	10
Worker	Public B	23·49	11
Clerk	Public B	23·00	12
Overall		26·28	

bigger size factories in the private and the public sectors only. Higher job status tended to contribute to greater adjustment to work. The analysis established that superior technology, bigger size of the unit, private ownership of the enterprise, and higher job status of an employee were associated with the employees' superior adjustment to work.

By Social Characteristics

So far, we have discussed the respondents' adjustment to work in its institutional context. We now turn to some of the personal and social attributes of the respondents that might have a bearing on their adjustment. For this purpose, employees' income, education and skill, age, origin, background, caste, previous employment, and dependency load were selected for analysis. Two kinds of analysis were made. First, respondents in each of the 27 sub-groups were grouped on different personal and social attributes, and their Mean Scores were obtained. This yielded comparative Mean Score figures of the respondents' adjustment to work by job status and by factory types. The associations between group scores and sub-group scores on each of the attributes were calculated by rank order method and the 'Rho' was worked out. Second, all the 462 respondents were divided into several sub-groups on different personal/social attributes, and their Mean Scores were compared with the Overall Mean Score (Mean=26·28, S.D.=8·37). The significance of difference between each sub-group Mean and the total Mean was determined by computing statistic 'Z'. The detailed results have been presented in Tables 12 to 20 given at the end of this chapter. A reference to the results has been made in the discussion at the appropriate places.

INCOME

All respondents were divided into three income groups, namely the lower (less than Rs. 100 per month), the middle (between Rs. 101 and 200 per month), and the upper (more than Rs. 201 per month).

TABLE 3

Table showing income and adjustment to work

Group	N	Mean	Critical value	P
Lower Rs. 100 and below	193	23·8	4·14	0·001
Middle Rs. 101 to Rs. 200	232	27·2	1·63	ns
Upper Rs. 201 and above	37	31·1	3·49	0·001

The Test of Association between adjustment to work and income of the lower, the middle, and the upper income groups yielded a value of 0·15, 0·45, and, 0·96 respectively. The Mean Score of each income group was very near to the overall Mean Score, showing the average level of adjustment. The Mean Score of the lower and the upper income groups varied considerably from the overall Mean Score, with the upper income group at 31·1 and the lower income group at 23·8. This shows a direct relationship between income and adjustment to work. Higher income was directly related with higher adjustment to work, and lower income generated very low adjustment to work. Thus, we find a linear relationship between the respondents' income and their adjustment to work (Table 20).

EDUCATION

The respondents were divided into three groups by the levels of their education. Those who had four years' schooling constituted the lower education group, those with 5 to 10 years' schooling the middle education group, and those who had more than 10 years' schooling the higher education group. The Mean Scores for each group were computed and are shown in Table 4.

TABLE 4

Table showing education and adjustment to work

Schooling group	N	Mean	Critical value	P
Lower	162	25·5	1·21	ns
Middle	192	25·7	0·99	ns
Higher	108	28·7	2·98	0·01

The association between education and adjustment to work of respondents was 0·09 for the lower education group, 0·108 for the middle education group, and 0·91 for the higher education group. The critical value of the difference between the Mean Score of the higher education group and the total Mean Score was large enough, while those of the remaining groups were too little to attain the level of significance. This shows that the employees with higher education were better adjusted than those with lower education. The same tendency prevailed in all types of factories except 'Public B' where the relationship was negative, *i.e.* higher education corresponded with lower scores and, thus, to a lower level of adjustment (Table 13).

SKILL

All respondents were divided into skilled and unskilled groups and the Mean Scores computed. The same are presented in Tables 5 and 14.

TABLE 5

Table showing skill and adjustment to work

Group	N	Mean	Critical value	P
Unskilled	193	24·4	3·15	0·01
Skilled	269	27·5	2·35	0·05

The respondents in the skilled group showed superior adjustment to work to that of those in the unskilled group. The Mean Score of the skilled group was significantly higher than the total Mean Score (critical value=2·35). The Mean Score of the unskilled group was significantly lower than the total Mean Score (critical value=3·15). These results were further supported by the Test of Association which yielded a negative value (of 0·087) with adjustment to work in the unskilled group. The respondents displayed a consistent tendency along these lines irrespective of the factory types.

AGE

The respondents were divided into two age groups, *viz.*, below 30 years and above 30 years, and the Test of Association performed. While it yielded an association ranging from 0·789 to 0·93 between age and adjustment to work, it did not discriminate between the age groups. However, in the case of respondents employed in private enterprises, the younger age group tended to be better adjusted (Mean 27·7) than the older age group (Mean 25·7). The reverse was true in the case of respondents belonging to 'Public B' type factories, where the older age employees were better adjusted (Mean 26·6) than the younger age group (Mean 23·00). Tables 6 and 12 show that the difference on the whole was not significant.

TABLE 6

Table showing age and adjustment to work

Group	N	Mean	Critical value	P
Below 30 years	295	26·5	0·41	ns
Above 30 years	167	25·8	0·77	ns

ORIGIN

The analysis on the basis of the employees' origin (rural *versus* urban) revealed negligible differences in their levels of adjustment. In both the groups there was almost an equal association (0·83 and 0·84) of origin with adjustment to work. The urban employees, however, tended to be better adjusted in the private enterprises (Tables 7 and 17).

TABLE 7

Table showing origin and adjustment to work

Group	N	Mean	Critical value	P
Rural	250	25·7	1·13	ns
Urban	212	27·1	1·39	ns

MIGRATION

The respondents were divided into three groups according to their place of origin. Those that belonged to Kota district were placed in the first group; those who came from the other districts of Rajasthan were included in the second group; and the rest who migrated from other States were put in the third group. The Test of Association revealed that in the case of the first two groups, there was negligible relationship between their migration and adjustment to work (Rho being 0.155 and 0.398 respectively). However, there was a significant association (Rho=0.787) between migration and adjustment to work of respondents in the third group. A comparison of the Mean Scores of the three groups also revealed that the third group had superior adjustment, yielding a critical value of 2.68. These results were consistent among all four factory types (Tables 8 and 16).

TABLE 8

Table showing migration and adjustment to work

Group	N	Mean	Critical value	P
Kota	132	25.00	1.78	ns
Rajasthan (other than Kota)	132	25.80	0.68	ns
Other States	198	27.90	2.68	0.01

CASTE

The first attempt to find the association between caste and adjustment to work of respondents proved futile due to the weaker strength of the three higher castes in the sample. Therefore, the respondents were divided into two caste groups only—Harijans and other castes. No perceptible differences were found from the analysis which could account for any influence of caste on adjustment to work of respondents (Tables 9 and 18).

TABLE 9

Table showing caste and adjustment to work

Group	N	Mean	Critical value	P
Harijans	91	26·5	0·22	ns
Other Castes	295	26·1	0·41	ns

PREVIOUS EMPLOYMENT EXPERIENCE

The respondents were divided into two groups on the basis of their experience of previous employment, namely those who had up to 2 years' experience, and those who had more than 2 years' experience. There was no difference in the Mean Scores of the two groups, showing the irrelevance of previous experience to adjustment to work. However, there was a tendency on the part of the more experienced employees to have superior adjustment in 'A' type factories while the reverse was true of those in 'B' type factories (Tables 10 and 15).

TABLE 10

Table showing previous employment experience and adjustment to work

Group	N	Mean	Critical value	P
Experience up to 2 years	43	26·2	0·07	ns
Experience of more than 2 years	205	26·1	0·17	ns

DEPENDENCY LOAD

All respondents were divided into two groups according to their dependency load. Those who had to support up to three persons were put into one group, and those who had more than three dependents formed the other group. It was found that the first group scored higher on the Job Attitude Scale in 'Private A' factories only. An analysis by factory types and the overall comparative results showed the ineffectiveness of this factor (Tables 11 and 19).

TABLE 11

Table showing dependency load and adjustment to work

Group	N	Mean	Critical value	P
1 to 3 members	220	26·0	0·53	ns
More than 3 members	214	26·7	0·69	ns

CONCLUSIONS

The results of the analysis presented in the foregoing pages bring out a few important conclusions. It was found that the employees' adjustment to work varied in descending order by factory types and by job status. It was the highest in 'Private A', followed by 'Public A', 'Private B', and 'Public B'. Further, in each of the factory types, the supervisors displayed superior adjustment to work as compared to the workers or the clerks (the latter two groups did not show any statistically significant differences). Thus, superior technology and bigger size (in terms of employment) of plants, and higher job status of workers were associated with superior adjustment to work of the employees. The nature of ownership of plants (private *versus* public sector) did not introduce any significant differences in the employees' levels of adjustment except in bigger size plants which used superior technology.

So far as the influence of the respondents' social characteristics on their adjustment to work was concerned, it was found that higher income, higher education, and higher skill were associated with employees' superior adjustment in each of the twelve groups. A linear relationship existed between an employee's adjustment to work and his education, income, and skill. The immigrants displayed work adjustment superior to that of the local or the Rajasthani employees, irrespective of job status and factory type. Age, caste, origin, work experience, and the dependency load of respondents influenced their adjustment to work in a differential pattern only. Younger age was associated with higher adjustment to work of the employees in 'Public A' and with lower adjustment in 'Public B'. Similarly, longer work experience was associated with higher adjustment to work of employees working in bigger plants, and with low adjustment in the case of those working in smaller size plants. The urbanites displayed higher adjustment to work in the private enterprises only.

We are now in a position to state the institutional as well as the personal determinants of the employees' adjustment to work. The technology involved in the production process and the size (in terms of employment) of the plants, and the job status of employees were the most important institutional determinants of their adjustment to work. Education, skill, income, and migratory status of workers were the major personal attributes that influenced the employees' adjustment to work. The employees' adjustment to work was not rooted in one single factor—either institutional or personal. Rather, it was sustained by a set of complex interactions and inter-relationships between work situations and personal attributes.

A proper ordering of interactions between the two forces, namely, the work situation and the personal attributes, is a *sine qua non* of the employees' adjustment to work. Superior plant technology requires higher skills that carry a correspondingly higher price. Very often, higher skills and greater earnings are also associated with higher education and higher job status. Thus, the matching of skills with technology becomes crucial to the employees' adjustment to work. Any drive to improve employees' adjustment to work must begin with an understanding of the social significance of the technology involved, the relationship between the machine and its operative, and the skill requirement.

Further, skill needs to be appropriately rewarded in terms of both money and status. The analysis points out to several policy implications for industrial undertakings, more particularly for recruitment and wage policies. A company that desires adjusted employees must match men with jobs and pay them wages that are commensurate with skills. In addition to proper selection and wages, it must also give recognition to employees by establishing job status that goes with skill and pay. The recruitment and wage policies of a company should establish that they recognize ability, skill, and merit, and that the company is happy to have such people and wishes to make their stay worthwhile.

TABLE 12

Table showing distribution of employees in the various age groups with their mean job satisfaction scores, by types, by nature and by size of factories and by job status also

Job status	Groups	Factory types							
		Private A		Public A		Private B		Public B	
		Below 30 Years	Above 30 Years	Below 30 Years	Above 30 Years	Below 30 Years	Above 30 Years	Below 30 Years	Above 30 Years
Workers	N=(In each group)	51	9	86	54	89	41	27	34
	M=(Mean Scores of each group)	29·3	26·3	25·6	26·0	25·5	24·0	22·2	24·5
Clerks	N=(In each group)	11	1	5	6	5	0	3	3
	M=(Mean Scores of each group)	29·3	37·0	26·2	23·8	27·8	—	22·3	23·6
Supervisors	N=(In each group)	5	2	5	5	5	7	3	5
	M=(Mean Scores of each group)	37·2	37·0	26·0	28·0	38·0	30·0	33·0	36·2
Total Employees	N=	67	12	96	65	99	48	33	42
	M=	29·3	29·0	24·6	25·9	26·3	25·0	23·0	26·6

Contd.

TABLE 12 (contd.)

| Job status | Groups | Nature of enterprises |||| Size of factory |||| Total of all factories ||
| | | Private sector || Public sector || A Type || B Type || | |
		Below 30 Years	Above 30 Years	Below 30 Years	Above 30 Years	Below 30 Years	Above 30 Years	Below 30 Years	Above 30 Years	Below 30 Years	Above 30 Years
Workers	N=(In each group)	140	50	113	88	137	63	116	75	253	138
	M=(Mean Scores of each group)	27·4	24·3	24·8	25·4	26·6	26·0	24·7	24·2	26·0	25·0
Clerks	N=(In each group)	16	1	8	9	16	7	8	3	24	10
	M=(Mean Scores of each group)	28·8	37·0	24·7	23·8	28·3	25·7	25·7	23·6	27·4	25·1
Supervisors	N=(In each group)	10	9	8	10	10	7	8	12	18	19
	M=(Mean Scores of each group)	37·5	31·5	28·5	32·1	31·6	30·6	35·9	32·6	33·5	31·8
Total Employees	N=	166	60	129	107	163	77	132	90	295	167
	M=	27·7	25·7	25·0	26·0	26·5	26·4	25·5	25·3	26·5	25·8

Test of Association for the age groups : Below 30 years = 0·93
Above 30 years = 0·789

TABLE 13

Table showing distribution of employees in the various educational groups with their mean job satisfaction scores, by types, by nature and by size of factories and by job status also

Job status	Groups	Private A 1	Private A 2	Private A 3	Public A 1	Public A 2	Public A 3	Private B 1	Private B 2	Private B 3	Public B 1	Public B 2	Public B 3
Workers	N=(In each group) M=(Mean Scores of each group)	20 27·3	21 29·2	18 32·8	37 25·9	77 25·3	26 27·0	75 24·9	52 26·5	3 18·3	28 25·3	27 23·3	6 20·6
Clerks	N=(In each group) M=(Mean Scores of each group)	0 —	0 —	12 29·9	0 —	3 28·0	8 23·7	0 —	1 38·0	4 25·2	0 —	1 26·0	5 22·4
Supervisors	N=(In each group) M=(Mean Scores of each group)	0 —	0 —	7 37·1	0 —	4 24·2	6 29·0	1 32·0	3 38·1	8 31·5	0 —	3 35·3	5 34·6
Total Employees	N= M=	20 27·3	21 29·2	37 32·7	37 25·9	84 25·3	40 26·7	76 25·0	56 29·1	15 27·2	28 25·3	31 29·1	16 25·6

Contd.

TABLE 13 (contd.)

Job status	Groups	Nature of enterprises						Size of factory									Total of all factories		
		Private sector			Public sector			A Type			B Type					
		1	2	3	1	2	3	1	2	3	1	2	3	1	2	3
Workers	N= (In each group)	95	73	21	65	104	32	57	98	44	103	79	9	160	177	53
	M= (Mean Scores of each group)	25·4	27·3	30·7	25·6	24·8	26·0	26·4	26·0	29·4	25·0	25·4	20·4	25·5	25·8	27·8
Clerks	N= (In each group)	0	1	16	0	4	13	0	3	20	0	2	9	0	5	29
	M= (Mean Scores of each group)	—	38·0	28·7	—	27·5	23·2	—	28·0	27·5	—	32·0	23·6	—	29·6	26·3
Supervisors	N= (In each group)	1	3	15	0	7	11	0	4	13	1	6	13	1	10	26
	M= (Mean Scores of each group)	32·0	38·1	34·1	—	30·3	31·4	—	24·2	33·3	32·0	36·8	33·0	32·0	32·7	33·0
Total Employees	N=	96	77	52	65	115	56	57	115	77	104	87	31	161	192	108
	M=	25·5	27·8	31·1	25·6	25·2	26·4	26·4	23·8	29·6	25·1	26·3	26·5	25·5	25·7	28·7

Test of Association for the educational groups :

Illiterate =0·09
Below Matric =0·108
Matric and above =0·91

Groups : 1=Illiterate
2=Below Matric
3=Above Matric

TABLE 14

Table showing distribution of employees in the unskilled and skilled groups with their mean job satisfaction scores, by types, by nature and by size of factories and by job status also

Job status	Groups	Private A 1	Private A 2	Public A 1	Public A 2	Private B 1	Private B 2	Public B 1	Public B 2
Workers	N=(In each group)	27	33	38	102	89	41	39	22
	M=(Mean Scores of each group)	25·3	31·8	24·5	26·4	24·7	25·8	23·2	23·9
Clerks	N=(In each group)	0	12	0	11	0	5	0	6
	M=(Mean Scores of each group)	—	29·9	—	24·9	—	27·8	—	23·0
Supervisors	N=(In each group)	0	7	0	10	0	12	0	8
	M=(Mean Scores of each group)	—	37·1	—	27·0	—	33·2	—	35·0
Total Employees	N=	27	52	38	123	89	58	39	36
	M=	25·3	32·1	24·5	26·1	24·7	27·5	23·2	26·2

Contd.

TABLE 14 (contd.)

| Job status | Groups | Nature of enterprises |||| Size of factory |||||| Total of all factories ||
| | | Private sector || Public sector || A Type || B Type || | |
		1	2	1	2	1	2	1	2	1	2
Workers	N = (In each group)	116	74	77	124	65	135	128	63	193	198
	M = (Mean Scores of each group)	24·8	28·5	23·9	25·8	24·8	27·5	24·4	25·2	24·4	26·8
Clerks	N = (In each group)	0	17	0	17	0	23	0	11	0	34
	M = (Mean Scores of each group)	—	29·3	—	24·2	—	27·5	—	25·2	—	26·7
Supervisors	N = (In each group)	0	19	0	18	0	17	0	20	0	37
	M = (Mean Scores of each group)	—	34·7	—	30·5	—	31·2	—	33·9	—	32·6
Total Employees	N =	116	110	77	159	65	175	128	94	193	269
	M =	24·8	29·7	23·9	26·1	24·8	27·9	24·4	27·0	24·4	27·5

Test of Association for the unskilled and skilled groups : Unskilled = 0·087
Skilled = 0·99

Groups : 1 = Unskilled
2 = Skilled

TABLE 15

Table showing distribution of employees in the two groups according to their previous employment experience and their mean job satisfaction scores, by types, by nature and by size of factories and by job status also

Job status	Groups	Private A 1	Private A 2	Public A 1	Public A 2	Private B 1	Private B 2	Public B 1	Public B 2
Workers	N = (In each group)	8	39	11	29	13	87	1	24
	M = (Mean Scores of each group)	26·5	29·3	22·4	26·0	27·0	24·4	20·0	23·3
Clerks	N = (In each group)	4	3	1	4	2	1	0	2
	M = (Mean Scores of each group)	24·7	32·3	28·0	24·2	30·0	38·0	—	21·5
Supervisors	N = (In each group)	1	4	0	3	2	7	0	2
	M = (Mean Scores of each group)	35·0	36·2	—	30·3	37·0	31·4	—	36·0
Total Employees	N =	13	46	12	36	17	95	1	28
	M =	26·6	30·1	22·8	26·1	28·6	25·0	20·0	23·3

Contd.

TABLE 15 (contd.)

Job status		Nature of enterprises				Size of factory				Total of all factories	
		Private sector		Public sector		A Type		B Type			
	Groups	1	2	1	2	1	2	1	2	1	2
Workers	N=(In each group)	21	126	12	53	19	68	14	111	33	179
	M=(Mean Scores of each group)	26·9	25·9	22·1	24·3	24·1	27·9	26·6	23·9	25·1	25·4
Clerks	N=(In each group)	6	4	1	6	5	7	2	3	7	10
	M=(Mean Scores of each group)	26·5	33·7	28·0	23·3	25·2	27·7	30·0	27·0	26·7	27·5
Supervisors	N=(In each group)	3	11	0	5	1	7	2	9	3	16
	M=(Mean Scores of each group)	36·3	33·2	—	32·6	35·0	33·7	37·0	32·4	36·3	33·0
Total Employees	N=	30	141	13	64	25	82	18	123	43	205
	M=	27·7	26·7	22·6	24·9	24·8	28·4	28·1	24·6	26·2	26·1

Test of Association for the two groups : Experience up to 2 years =0·448   Groups : 1 = Up to 2 years
Experience for more than 2 years =0·875   2 = More than 2 years

TABLE 16

Table showing distribution of employees in the various groups by their origin and their mean job satisfaction scores, by types, by nature and by size of factories and by job status also

Job status	Groups	Private A 1	Private A 2	Private A 3	Public A 1	Public A 2	Public A 3	Private B 1	Private B 2	Private B 3	Public B 1	Public B 2	Public B 3
Workers	N = (In each group) M = (Mean Scores of each group)	20 27·4	17 25·5	23 32·2	12 22·6	51 26·4	77 25·9	32 23·9	16 24·7	32 27·1	49 23·6	7 24·1	5 24·4
Clerks	N = (In each group) M = (Mean Scores of each group)	4 38·5	1 40·0	7 26·4	3 21·0	3 30·3	5 24·0	2 32·0	3 25·0	0 —	4 23·2	1 28·0	1 17·0
Supervisors	N = (In each group) M = (Mean Scores of each group)	0 —	0 —	7 37·1	1 25·0	2 30·0	8 26·4	2 25·5	1 34·0	9 35·6	3 35·3	0 —	5 34·6
Total Employees	N = M =	24 29·2	18 26·3	37 32·1	16 22·4	56 26·8	89 25·8	86 24·4	60 24·8	61 28·2	56 24·2	8 24·4	11 28·3

Contd.

TABLE 16 (*contd.*)

Job status	Groups	Nature of enterprises							Size of factory										Total of all factories		
		Private sector			Public sector			A Type			B Type								
		1	2	3	1	2	3	1	2	3	1	2	3	1	2	3
Workers	N= (In each group)	52	63	75	61	68	82	32	68	100	81	53	67	113	121	157
	M= (Mean Scores of each group)	25·2	24·8	28·6	23·4	26·1	25·8	25·6	26·2	27·4	23·7	24·5	26·8	24·2	25·5	27·1
Clerks	N= (In each group)	6	4	7	7	4	6	7	4	12	6	4	1	13	8	13
	M= (Mean Scores of each group)	36·3	28·7	26·4	22·3	29·7	23·0	31·0	32·7	25·4	26·2	25·8	17·0	28·7	29·2	24·7
Supervisors	N= (In each group)	2	1	16	4	2	12	1	2	14	5	1	14	6	3	28
	M= (Mean Scores of each group)	25·5	34·0	35·8	32·7	30·0	29·8	25·0	30·0	31·8	31·4	34·0	34·8	30·3	31·3	33·3
Total Employees	N= M=	60 26·3	68 25·2	98 29·6	72 24·1	64 26·5	100 26·1	40 26·5	74 26·6	126 27·6	92 24·3	58 25·0	72 28·2	132 25·0	132 25·8	198 27·9

Test of Association for the three groups by origin :
    Kota group =0·155
    Rajasthan group =0·398
    Group from other States =0·767

Groups : 1 = Kota
             2 = Rajasthan
             3 = Other States

TABLE 17

Table showing distribution of employees in the rural-urban groups with their mean job satisfaction scores, by types, by nature and by size of factories and by job status also

Job status		Groups	Private A Rural	Private A Urban	Public A Rural	Public A Urban	Private B Rural	Private B Urban	Public B Rural	Public B Urban
Workers	N=(In each group)		43	17	74	66	82	48	24	37
	M=(Mean Scores of each group)		27·3	32·2	26·05	25·55	23·8	28·3	25·8	22·4
Clerks	N=(In each group)		3	9	6	5	4	1	1	5
	M=(Mean Scores of each group)		28·3	30·4	24·6	25·2	25·2	38·0	17·0	24·2
Supervisors	N=(In each group)		1	6	4	6	6	6	2	6
	M=(Mean Scores of each group)		35·0	37·5	23·0	26·3	35·2	31·3	35·0	35·0
Total Employees	N=		47	32	84	77	92	55	27	48
	M=		27·5	32·7	25·8	25·5	24·6	28·8	26·1	24·1

Contd.

TABLE 17 (contd.)

Job status	Groups	Nature of enterprises				Size of factory				Total of all factories	
		Private sector		Public sector		A Type		B Type			
		Rural	Urban	Rural	Urban	Rural	Urban	Rural	Urban	Rural	Urban
Workers	N = (In each group)	125	65	98	103	117	83	106	85	223	168
	M = (Mean Scores of each group)	25·0	27·3	26·4	24·5	26·5	26·9	24·2	25·7	25·4	26·3
Clerks	N = (In each group)	7	10	7	10	9	14	5	6	14	20
	M = (Mean Scores of each group)	26·6	31·2	23·6	24·7	26·0	28·5	23·6	26·5	25·0	28·0
Supervisors	N = (In each group)	7	12	6	12	5	12	8	12	13	24
	M = (Mean Scores of each group)	35·1	34·4	27·0	30·6	25·4	32·0	35·0	33·1	31·4	32·5
Total Employees	N =	139	87	111	125	131	109	119	103	250	212
	M =	25·6	30·2	25·9	25·0	26·4	27·7	25·0	26·6	25·7	27·1

Test of Association for the rural-urban groups : Rural = 0·83
Urban = 0·846

TABLE 18

Table showing distribution of employees in the various caste groups with their mean job satisfaction scores, by types, by nature and by size of factories and by job status also

Job status	Groups	Private A 1	Private A 2	Public A 1	Public A 2	Private B 1	Private B 2	Public B 1	Public B 2
Workers	N=(In each group) M=(Mean Scores of each group)	18 28·1	36 29·6	39 26·1	76 24·9	14 26·0	91 24·9	7 25·1	44 23·0
Clerks	N=(In each group) M=Mean Scores of each group)	4 27·0	7 31·8	3 20·6	7 26·3	1 27·0	4 28·0	1 28·0	5 22·0
Supervisors	N=(In each group) M=(Mean Scores of each group)	2 37·0	4 37·7	0 —	7 28·0	0 —	9 34·3	2 36·5	5 34·2
Total Employees	N= M=	24 28·7	47 30·6	42 25·7	90 25·2	15 24·7	104 25·9	10 27·7	54 24·0

Contd.

TABLE 18 (contd.)

Job status	Groups	Nature of enterprises				Size of factory				Total of all factories	
		Private sector		Public sector		A Type		B Type			
		1	2	1	2	1	2	1	2	1	2
Workers	N=(In each group)	32	127	46	120	57	112	21	135	78	247
	M=(Mean Scores of each group)	26·5	26·2	26·0	24·2	26·7	24·4	25·2	25·0	26·2	25·2
Clerks	N=(In each group)	5	11	4	12	7	14	2	9	9	23
	M=(Mean Scores of each group)	27·0	30·4	22·5	24·5	24·3	29·0	27·5	24·6	25·0	27·3
Supervisors	N=(In each group)	2	13	2	12	2	11	2	14	4	25
	M=(Mean Scores of each group)	37·0	35·4	36·5	30·6	37·0	31·5	36·5	34·3	36·7	33·0
Total Employees	N=	39	151	52	144	66	137	25	153	91	295
	M=	27·1	27·3	26·1	24·8	20·7	27·1	26·0	25·2	26·5	26·1

Test of Association for the caste groups : Harijans = 0·38
Other castes = 0·97

Groups : 1 = Harijans
2 = Other castes

TABLE 19

Table showing distribution of employees in the two groups according to dependency load, with their mean job satisfaction scores by types, by nature and by size of factories and by job status also

Job status		Factory types								
		Private A		Public A		Private B		Public B		
	Groups	1	2	1	2	1	2	1	2
Workers	N=(In each group)	31	26	67	69	68	51	29	29
	M=(Mean Scores of each group)	28·0	30·6	25·9	25·5	25·6	24·7	21·7	25·1
Clerks	N=(In each group)	4	7	7	4	3	1	2	4
	M=(Mean Scores of each group)	30·5	31·0	25·7	23·5	32·6	27·0	27·0	21·0
Supervisors	N=(In each group)	0	7	2	7	3	7	4	2
	M=(Mean Scores of each group)	—	37·1	30·5	27·6	37·3	32·3	34·2	37·0
Total Employees	N=	35	40	76	80	74	59	35	35
	M=	28·2	31·8	28·0	28·6	28·4	25·6	23·4	25·3

Contd.

TABLE 19 (*contd.*)

Job status		Nature of enterprises				Size of factory				Total of all factories	
		Private sector		Public sector		A Type		B Type			
	Groups	1	2	1	2	1	2	1	2	1	2
Workers	N=(In each group)	99	77	96	98	98	95	97	80	195	175
	M=(Mean Scores of each group)	26·3	26·7	24·6	25·4	26·3	26·9	24·3	24·9	25·5	26·0
Clerks	N=(In each group)	7	8	9	8	11	11	5	5	16	16
	M=(Mean Scores of each group)	31·4	30·5	26·0	22·2	27·4	28·2	30·4	22·2	28·4	26·4
Supervisors	N=(In each group)	3	14	6	9	2	14	7	9	9	23
	M=(Mean Scores of each group)	37·3	34·7	33·0	29·6	30·5	38·3	35·6	33·3	34·4	32·7
Total Employees	N=	109	99	111	115	111	120	109	94	220	214
	M=	27·0	28·1	25·2	25·5	26·7	27·6	25·4	25·6	26·0	26·7

Test of Association for the dependency groups : Having 1 to 3 members ≑ 0·42
Having more than 3 members = 0·91

Groups : 1 = 1 to 3 members
2 = 4 members and above

TABLE 20

Table showing distribution of employees in the various income groups with their mean job satisfaction scores, by types, by nature and by size of factories and by job status also

Job status		Groups	Private A 1	Private A 2	Private A 3	Public A 1	Public A 2	Public A 3	Private B 1	Private B 2	Private B 3	Public B 1	Public B 2	Public B 3
Workers	N = (In each group)		26	29	5	39	100	1	88	39	3	37	24	0
	M = (Mean Scores of each group)		26·2	30·6	33·0	25·3	25·9	23·0	24·2	27·1	21·3	21·6	26·4	—
Clerks	N = (In each group)		0	10	2	0	11	0	2	2	1	0	6	0
	M = (Mean Scores of each group)		—	30·3	28·0	—	24·9	—	26·0	30·5	26·0	—	23·0	—
Supervisors	N = (In each group)		0	0	7	0	2	8	1	7	4	0	2	6
	M = (Mean Scores of each group)		—	—	37·1	—	30·5	26·1	34·0	32·4	34·5	—	34·5	35·0
Total Employees	N =		26	39	14	39	113	9	91	48	8	37	32	6
	M =		26·2	30·5	34·3	25·3	25·9	25·9	24·4	28·1	28·5	21·6	26·3	35·0

Contd.

TABLE 20 (contd.)

| Job status | Groups | Nature of enterprises ||||||| Size of factory ||||||| Total of all factories |||
| | | Private sector ||| Public sector ||| A Type ||| B Type ||| | | |
		1	2	3	1	2	3	1	2	3	1	2	3	1	2	3
Workers	N= (In each group)	114	68	8	76	124	1	65	129	6	125	63	3	190	192	9
	M= (Mean Scores of each group)	24·7	28·6	23·5	23·5	26·0	23·0	25·5	27·0	31·3	23·5	26·3	21·3	24·2	27·0	28·0
Clerks	N= (In each group)	2	12	3	0	17	0	0	21	2	2	8	1	2	29	3
	M= (Mean Scores of each group)	26·0	30·3	37·3	—	24·2	—	—	27·5	28·0	26·0	25·0	26·0	26·0	26·7	27·3
Super-visors	N= (In each group)	1	7	11	0	4	14	0	2	15	1	9	10	1	11	25
	M= (Mean Scores of each group)	34·0	32·4	36·2	—	32·5	30·0	—	30·5	31·2	34·0	32·6	34·8	34·0	32·4	32·7
Total Employees	N= M=	117 24·8	87 29·2	22 32·2	76 23·5	144 26·0	15 29·4	65 25·5	152 27·1	23 31·0	128 23·6	80 27·3	14 31·3	193 24·3	232 27·2	37 31·5

Test of Association for the income groups : Rs. 100 and below : Lower group=0·15
Rs. 101 to Rs. 200 : Middle group=0·45
Rs. 201 and above : Upper group=0·96

Groups : 1 = Lower
2 = Middle
3 = Upper

Chapter VI

THE IMAGE OF WORK

Introduction

In the preceding chapter, we analyzed the influence of the institutional factors and the social characteristics of employees on their adjustment to work. This chapter deals with the effect of selected job aspects on employees' adjustment to work. The job aspects selected for analysis include wages, job security, opportunity for advancement, housing, supervisors, work group, and working conditions. The selection of the job aspects was done on the basis of a pilot study.

The analysis reported here relates to the workers' group only (supervisors and clerks have been excluded). It is based upon three types of worker responses on each of the job aspects, namely, the respondents' *Expectations*, *Perceptions*, and *Reactions* (E, P, and R). The 'Expectation' refers to the order of priority of *what* a respondent wanted most in his job. The 'Perception' refers to *how* he viewed and rated what was good in his job. The 'Reaction' was his attitude arising out of the interaction between the expectation and the perception on a particular job aspect.

In order to know his expectations, every respondent was asked to consider a list of the selected job aspects and to choose the one that he wanted most in his job. Thereafter, he was asked to repeat the consideration of the list till he arranged all the seven job aspects in the order from the 'most wanted' to the 'least wanted'. The same procedure was followed for determining the range of his perceptions from the 'best' perceived to the 'worst' perceived in his job. The ranking of 'Reaction' was determined by analyzing item responses to the same seven job aspects in Part B of the questionnaire appended at the end. The E, P, and R responses so obtained were processed by factory types. The results have been given in Tables 1 to 4 (appended to this chapter).

The Results

Workers' Expectations

The workers' expectations and the order of priority as to what they wanted most in their jobs are presented in Table 1. It was found that they regarded wages as the most important aspect of the job. Many considerations weighed with them in their selection of jobs. But wages was their primary consideration. Whether they worked in a big plant or in a small mill, in a public sector undertaking or in a private enterprise, in an assembly shed or in a workshop, they wanted higher wages more than anything else. All the respondents in 'Private A', 96·5 per cent in 'Private B', and 93·1 per cent each in both 'Public A' and 'Public B' assigned first rank to wages.

Housing was assigned the second rank by 51·6 per cent of the respondents. An analysis by the nature of ownership of factories revealed that, whereas over half of the respondents in private enterprises wanted housing next only to wages, almost an equal number in public undertakings assigned third rank to it. The respondents belonging to 'Public A' gave second rank to opportunity for advancement, and those of 'Public B' to job security. As noted in Chapter II, 'Public A' had built a big housing colony for its workers. The majority of respondents in 'Public B' belonged to Kota. Thus, neither of these groups faced any pressing problem for housing. The respondents of private enterprises were faced with an acute housing problem in the absence of any provision by the factories. Available housing facilities in the town as well as new construction had lagged far behind requirements. This resulted in the respondents often renting unsatisfactory dwellings at high rates and that too after a long search. Therefore, the significance attached to housing by this category is not surprising. It merely points to the need for according high priority to housing in new growth centres.

Though job security got an overall third rank, noticeable differences were found in the order of priority indicated on this job aspect by the respondents belonging to different factory types. The workers in 'Public A' did not attach much importance to it. They were governed by rules akin to those of the civil service under which their jobs were virtually fully secure. The respondents working in 'Public B' considered job security as the second most important job factor. The explanation for this priority lies in the manner of growth of such services. The utilities are administered by the State government. The respondents in the utilities originally belonged to different princely State services which were in the process of integration at the time of the study and, therefore, were apprehensive of the future. The respondents in private enterprises considered job security next only to wages and housing, irrespective of the size of the plant for which they worked.

It has been stated earlier that whereas the respondents employed in 'Public A' assigned second rank to opportunities for advancement, those in 'Public B' and in the private enterprises did not attach much importance to this. We know from Chapter II that 'Public A' offered very few opportunities for promotion due to little labour turnover, limited expansion, and seniority considerations. On the other hand, the employees in 'Public B' were mostly of local origin, relatively less qualified, and knew that their companies had little to offer in this respect. Their desire to work at Kota and the consciousness of their limited qualifications made them less ambitious so far as promotions were concerned. They did not expect much from the companies. The private enterprises generally followed the policy of promoting employees on the basis of merit and many of them were expanding. Their employees saw ample opportunities for advancement in their jobs and consequently did not attach much importance to this factor. Supervisors, work group, and working conditions constituted the three least important job expectations for workers. Supervisors were given the least importance by the respondents in the private enterprises, and working conditions by those in public undertakings.

The analysis presented above gives a clear picture of the job expectations of workers at Kota. A worker in the Kota job market attached the greatest importance to wages. If he were offered employment in a private enterprise of any type, housing and job security would be his additional considerations. If he were to consider a position in 'Public A' type factory, next to wages he would look for opportunities of advancement, followed by housing. In 'Public B' type factories, he would look for job security along with higher wages.

Workers' Perceptions

The workers' perceptions of *what* was good in their jobs and the rating from the 'best' to the 'worst' of the seven job aspects by factory types have been shown in Table 2. It will be observed from the table that the respondents' perceptions of the job aspects stood in sharp contrast to their expectations of them. The employees of 'Private A' stated that supervisors were the best out of all job aspects. This was closely followed by work group. Job security and wages received third and fourth rank respectively. As this company provided no housing, the workers did not respond at all to this job aspect. The perceptions of the respondents in 'Private B' generally followed the pattern of those in 'Private A', except that the former group viewed their wages more unfavourably than the latter. The employees in 'Public A' perceived job security to be the best part of their employment. Wages were perceived as the worst, next lowest being the opportunity for advancement. They saw the supervisors, the work group and job security as the three best aspects of their jobs. The perceptions of the employees in 'Public B' followed the same pattern insofar as the best job aspects were concerned. However, this group viewed the opportunities for advancement as the worst part of their jobs. The perceptions relating to wages were also bad, but better than those in 'Public A'.

The perceptions of workers employed in private enterprises differed sharply from those of the public undertakings. All respondents perceived their wages as bad. But the importance of this perception lies in an inter-factory type difference. The employees of 'Public A' and 'Private B' viewed wages as the worst part of their jobs. The respondents working in 'Private A' perceived their wages to be the fourth best aspect of their jobs. Job security was seen as the best part of their jobs by persons working in public undertakings. However, this job aspect was regarded only the third best by the respondents in private enterprises. Opportunities for advancement and working conditions were perceived badly by all respondents, irrespective of the factory types they were employed in.

Thus, we find that all workers perceived that the supervisors and the work group were the best part of their jobs and the opportunities for advancement and the working conditions as the least good. They differed in their perceptions of other aspects of their jobs. Wages were generally perceived unfavourably, more in the public undertakings and to a much less extent in 'Private A'. Job security was seen as the best job aspect by those who were employed in public undertakings. The respondents in private enterprises perceived this as one of the three best job aspects.

Workers' Reactions

The workers' reactions to, and the rank order of their responses for, job aspects have been given in Table 3. On the whole, workers approved of their working conditions, work group, and security of employment. They disapproved wages, housing, and opportunities for advancement. The supervisors were neither approved nor disapproved of strongly. The differences in the respondents' approval of the job aspects became obvious when analyzed by factory types. The respondents belonging to 'Private A' strongly disapproved their factories' policy of not providing residential accommodation to employees. The wage policy was also censured. Further, they felt that job security was not adequate, and expressed their disapproval. The respondents approved of their work group, working conditions, and supervisors, and thereby appreciated the recruitment policy, and the supervisory and employment practices. In 'Public A', the respondents evaluated job security and housing policy most favourably and wages and promotion policy most unfavourably. The working conditions and supervisory practices were generally appreciated. In 'Private B', the wages and the provisions regarding employment security were strongly censured. The respondents in 'Public B' strongly disapproved of their housing conditions and wage levels. They appreciated security of employment, recruitment practices, and working conditions.

Discrepancy in Responses

The discrepancy in the workers' E, P, and R responses on the job aspects by factory types have been presented in Table 4. We find that the workers were dissatisfied with the wage levels in all factories. Excepting 'Private A', very high expectations on wages were accompanied by very low perceptions and most unfavourable reactions. In the former case, the discrepancy among E, P, and R was relatively less, which showed relatively less dissatisfaction. Likewise, all workers were indifferent to their working conditions and satisfied with their work group. The respondents belonging to private enterprises were satisfied with supervisory practices but those in public undertakings were indifferent to them. Housing was a source of dissatisfaction to all workers excepting those employed in 'Public A'. But the latter group was dissatisfied with the promotion opportunities available to them; as regards all other employees the discrepancies were not significant. So far as job security was concerned, the respondents employed in private enterprises were dissatisfied and those in public undertakings were satisfied with it.

On the whole, the respondents were dissatisfied with wage levels and housing conditions. They were satisfied with the recruitment practices, were moderately satisfied with the provisions of job security, and were indifferent to working conditions and supervisory practices.

Conclusions

We are now in a position to sum up the results of the analysis presented in this chapter, and to bring out their implications for enterprises. The results pertain to workers' expectations, perceptions, and reactions. The extent of the discrepancy among the three (E, P, and R) indicates the degree of workers' dissatisfaction with their jobs.

What did the workers want most in their jobs?[1] The results provide the following answer.

All Workers : wages, housing, job security, and opportunity for advancement

Workers by Factory Types :
  Private A : wages, housing, job security, and opportunity for advancement
  Public A : wages, opportunity for advancement, housing, and job security
  Private B : wages, housing, job security, and opportunity for advancement
  Public B : wages, job security, housing, and opportunity for advancement

What did the workers perceive as 'good' in their jobs? The statement furnished below provides the answer to the question.

All Workers: work group, supervisors, job security, and wages

Workers by Factory Types :
  Private A : supervisors, work group, job security, and wages
  Public A : job security, work group, supervisors and housing
  Private B : work group, supervisors, job security, and housing

[1] The job aspects are listed in the order of their priority to the respondents.

Public B : job security, work group, supervisors, and working conditions

The third set of findings pertain to workers' attitudes towards the different aspects of their jobs. What did they find satisfactory in their jobs? Their answers are stated below in the order from the 'most' to the 'least' satisfying.

All Workers: working conditions, work group, job security, and supervisors

Workers by Factory Types:
Private A : work group, working conditions, and supervisors
Public A : job security, housing, and working conditions
Private B : working conditions, work group, and supervisors
Public B : job security, work group, and working conditions

We find that the workers had low expectations for work group, working conditions, and supervisors. Therefore, their satisfaction on these items might not be taken as a positive attitude. These job aspects were just not important to them.

The workers in the public undertakings were satisfied with job security. They expressed it as one of the 'most wanted' aspects of jobs, found it good and, therefore, approved their companies' policies in this respect. On balance, how did the workers evaluate their companies' policies? We find that the workers employed in 'Private A' were dissatisfied with their company's wages and housing policies, and were satisfied with recruitment policies, supervisory practices, and working conditions. In 'Public A', the workers were dissatisfied with the wages and promotion policies, were satisfied with the housing programmes and job security, and were indifferent to other things. The workers in 'Private B' expressed dissatisfaction with the wage policies and the provisions for job security, while those in 'Public B' disapproved the wages and the housing policies of their companies.

The summary of the results as given above lead us to suggest a few implications for company policies. First, it throws sufficient light on what will attract workers to a company, and on the manner in which the process of job selection operates in the minds of workers. We find that workers attach the greatest importance to wages. They are most likely to be attracted by a job that offers the highest remuneration (other things are important but only secondary). Having considered wages in a job, a worker turns to weigh other aspects of the job. Confronted with a choice of being employed in a private enterprise or a public undertaking, he will look for job security in the former and promotion opportunities in the latter. An offer of a job at a place like Kota will be less attractive unless it is accompanied by a provision for residential accommodation. Supervisory practices, working conditions, and work group, important though they are, do not find much weight in workers' thought processes at the time of evaluating the possibility of employment in a particular plant at Kota.

Second, apart from the importance of wages, the analysis sheds light on the workers' feelings about it. They were generally dissatisfied with their wages. This is what could be expected under conditions of continuous increase in the cost of living. However, they did distinguish between good wages and wages. We observed relatively less dissatisfaction on this account in 'Private A' where wage rates were relatively higher. This only shows that a progressive wage policy is bound to be recognized by workers whatever be the cost of living.

Third, we are presented with a profile of the ambitions of a new worker. He wants more wages and better housing. He is ambitious and seeks the job that offers opportunities to move up. He is young and literate. The land back home did not treat him well. He has come to a new place in search of better prospects. Labour legislation enables him to secure better working conditions; and he takes it for granted. The companies work hard to develop good recruitment policies and supervisory practices. But he does not seem to attach much importance to them. These things are low on his priority scale. We do not know enough about the causes for these attitudes. Perhaps, being a new worker, he is ignorant of matters that are outside his immediate interests and needs; his personal goals of earning a good living motivate him so strongly as to urge him to disregard everything that does not serve this end directly.

Finally, the analysis points out to the need for improving employment security practices in private enterprises and to the reconsideration of promotion policies in public undertakings. Good wages, housing, job security, and promotion opportunities are the four job aspects that are wanted most by all workers.

Before concluding, we would like to draw attention to the role of technology in workers' adjustment to work. We know from the preceding chapter that to the extent that technology determined skill requirements of a plant, it also determined employees' earnings, education, and job status. A higher wage was the most wanted job aspect. Since higher earnings are possible, by and large, in plants that use superior technology, we are led to comment that those who expect to earn higher wages must move to plants using superior technology. Since the desire to earn more is universal—as the results show—, we could expect workers to move from simple technology plants to superior technology plants. Alternatively, they may move from one region to another, depending upon the technology involved in the production processes of plants located at such places.

TABLE 1

Table showing responses and relative rankings of employees' expectations in regard to certain job factors by types, by nature and by size of factories

Job factors	Private A %	Private A Rank	Public A %	Public A Rank	Private B %	Private B Rank	Public B %	Public B Rank
Wages	100·0	1	93·1	1	96·1	1	93·1	1
Job Security	31·7	3	47·6	4	50·7	3	52·3	2
Opportunity for Advancement	23·3	4	59·0	2	31·6	4	47·0	4
Housing	56·8	2	50·0	3	53·0	2	48·0	3
Supervisors	5·0	7	11·0	5	3·0	6	13·0	6
Work Group	8·3	6	5·5	6	6·9	5	21·2	5
Working Conditions	13·0	5	2·8	7	2·4	7	10·0	7

Contd.

TABLE 1 (contd.)

| Job factors | Nature of enterprises |||| Size of factories |||||| Total of all factories ||
| | Private sector || Public sector || A Type || B Type || | |
	%	Rank	%	Rank	%	Rank	%	Rank	%	Rank
Wages	96·5	1	93·0	1	95·0	1	95·3	1	95·1	1
Job Security	44·7	3	48·8	4	42·5	4	51·3	2·5	46·8	3
Opportunity for Advancement	28·9	4	57·2	2	50·0	3	36·6	4	43·4	4
Housing	49·3	2	50·0	3	52·0	2	51·3	2·5	51·6	2
Supervisors	3·5	7	11·9	5	9·5	5	6·3	6	8·0	6
Work Group	7·4	5	8·7	6	5·5	6·5	11·5	5	8·2	5
Working Conditions	5·5	6	4·9	7	6·0	6·5	4·7	7	5·3	7

TABLE 2

Table showing responses and relative rankings of employees' perceptions of certain job factors by types, by nature and by size of factories

Job factors	Private A %	Private A Rank	Public A %	Public A Rank	Private B %	Private B Rank	Public B %	Public B Rank
Wages	6.6	4	9.5	7	10.2	6.5	4.5	5
Job Security	8.3	3	33.5	1	14.5	3	24.7	1
Opportunity for Advancement	3.3	5.5	10.5	6	9.5	6.5	3.0	6
Housing	—	—	21.6	4	13.0	4	—	—
Supervisors	35.0	1	26.5	3	28.9	2	12.5	3
Work Group	33.3	2	31.5	2	29.9	1	16.0	2
Working Conditions	3.3	5.5	13.5	5	11.5	5	6.5	4

Contd.

TABLE 2 (contd.)

Job factors	Nature of enterprises				Size of factories				Total of all factories	
	Private sector		Public sector		A Type		B Type			
	%	Rank	%	Rank	%	Rank	%	Rank	%	Rank
Wages	10·3	4	17·4	4	9·0	6·5	8·9	5	15·4	4
Job Security	13·1	3	30·9	1	26·0	3	12·6	3	20·0	3
Opportunity for Advancement	7·8	7	8·6	7	8·5	6·5	7·3	6·5	7·8	7
Housing	9·3	5·5	15·4	5	14·5	4	7·9	6·5	12·0	5
Supervisors	30·4	1·5	21·4	3	28·0	2	23·0	2	25·5	2
Work Group	30·3	1·5	26·7	2	37·0	1	25·7	1	28·8	1
Working Conditions	9·3	5·5	11·6	6	10·5	5	9·9	4	10·2	6

TABLE 3

Table showing responses and relative rankings of employees' reactions to certain job factors by types, by nature and by size of factories

Job factors	Private A %	Private A Rank	Public A %	Public A Rank	Private B %	Private B Rank	Public B %	Public B Rank
Wages	18·3	6	41·4	7	39·2	7	31·1	6
Job Security	46·5	5	88·6	1	40·8	6	85·2	1
Opportunity for Advancement	61·1	4	43·8	6	52·1	4	44·3	5
Housing	13·3	7	79·2	2	49·2	5	3·3	7
Supervisors	68·9	3	55·4	4	57·2	3	44·9	4
Work Group	90·0	1	49·3	5	67·7	2	78·7	2
Working Conditions	87·2	2	57·6	3	75·9	1	73·7	3

[*Contd.*

TABLE 3 (contd.)

Job factors	Nature of enterprises				Size of factories				Total of all factories	
	Private sector		Public sector		A Type		B Type			
	%	Rank	%	Rank	%	Rank	%	Rank	%	Rank
Wages	32·6	7	38·3	7	34·5	7	12·6	7	35·5	7
Job Security	42·6	5	87·6	1	76·0	1	55·0	3	65·0	3
Opportunity for Advancement	54·9	4	43·9	6	49·0	6	49·5	5	49·2	5
Housing	37·9	6	56·2	4	59·5	4·5	34·6	6	47·3	6
Supervisors	60·9	3	51·9	5	59·8	4·5	52·5	4	56·2	4
Work Group	74·7	2	58·2	3	61·5	3	71·1	2	66·2	2
Working Conditions	79·4	1	62·5	2	66·5	2	75·2	1	70·8	1

TABLE 4

Table showing discrepancy in employees' expectation, perception and reaction in ranking of certain job factors by nature, by size and by types of factories

Job factors	Private A E	Private A P	Private A R	Public A E	Public A P	Public A R	Private B E	Private B P	Private B R	Public B E	Public B P	Public B R
Wages	1	4	6	1	7	7	1	6	5·7	1	5	6
Job Security	3	3	5	4	1	1	3	3	6	2	1	1
Opportunity for Advancement	4	5·5	4	2	6	6	4	6·5	4	4	6	5
Housing	2	7	7	3	4	2	2	4	5	3	7	7
Supervisors	7	1	3	5	3	4	6	2	3	6	3	4
Work Group	6	2	1	6	2	5	5	1	2	5	2	2
Working Conditions	5	5·5	2	7	5	3	7	5	1	7	4	3

Contd.

TABLE 4 (contd.)

Job factors	Nature of enterprises						Size of factories						Total of all factories		
	Private sector			Public sector			A Type			B Type					
	E	P	R	E	P	R	E	P	R	E	P	R	E	P	R
Wages	1	4	7	1	4	7	1	6·5	7	1	5	7	1	4	7
Job Security	3	3	5	4	1	1	4	3	1	2·5	3	3	3	3	3
Opportunity for Advancement	4	7	4	2	7	6	3	6·5	6	4	6·5	5	4	7	5
Housing	2	5·5	6	3	5	4	2	4	4·5	2·5	6·5	6	2	5	6
Supervisors	7	1·5	3	5	3	5	5	2	4·5	6	2	4	6	2	4
Work Group	5	1·5	2	6	2	3	6·5	1	3	5	1	2	5	1	2
Working Conditions	6	5·5	1	7	6	2	6·5	5	2	7	4	1	7	6	1

CHAPTER VII

THE FINDINGS AND THEIR IMPLICATIONS

THE study presented in the preceding chapters provides an insight into the problems and processes of human adjustment to industrial work and the technology; and focusses attention on some of the factors that influence this adjustment. The study is based on interviews with employees undergoing the process of adjustment. The findings have relevance to Kota and similar other growth centres in the country. Hopefully, the study contributes to our understanding of the human aspects of the process of industrialization, and will help managements in determining strategies of human resources development, establishing appropriate policies of wages and fringe benefits, and generally to take steps to improve labour discipline and productivity.

THE FINDINGS

The investigation was guided by a number of specific questions raised in Chapter I.

Institutional Factors

It was hypothesized that the technology used in the production process, the size and ownership of a plant, and the job status of employees, were correlated with the human adjustment to work. The study brings out that employees working in plants that adopted superior technology—machine control operations and semi-automated processes—and were of larger size, displayed a higher level of adjustment to work than those working in assembly line operations or in utilities or in smaller size plants. The higher job status of employees tended to contribute to their greater adjustment to work. Supervisors were better adjusted than either workers or clerks. There did not exist much differences between the adjustment levels of workers and clerks. The ownership of an enterprise was significant to the employees' adjustment in the bigger size establishments only. The employees of the large private enterprise were better adjusted to work than those employed in the large public undertaking. There was no significant difference by ownership between the levels of adjustment of employees working in smaller enterprises.

Job Factors

It was also hypothesized that an employee's favourable reaction to his job would lead him to better adjustment to work. Since the reaction is a function of expectation-perception discrepancy (EPD), it was contended that an employee's adjustment to work was inversely correlated with his EPD. In the absence of a rating scale of total job aspects, correlations were worked out for only seven selected job aspects. It was found that the EPD was the highest with regard to wages irrespective of the factory type and size and ownership of enterprises. The workers were also found to be the least satisfied with wages. Again, all workers were indifferent to the working conditions but were satisfied with their work group. Further, workers belonging to private enterprises were satisfied with supervisory practices but those in public undertakings were indifferent to them. The EPD was high on housing for all workers except those employed in 'Public A'. The former were also found dissatisfied with the housing provisions. However, the latter group revealed a high EPD and expressed a greater dissatisfaction with the promotion opportunities available to them. The EPD was high on 'job security' in the case of workers employed in private enterprises whereas they expressed less satisfaction on this item on the whole. The EPD was very high on wage levels and housing conditions, significant on job security, and not significant on working conditions and supervisory practices. The study also shows that workers expressed the highest dissatisfaction on their wage levels and housing conditions, dissatisfaction on job security, indifference to working conditions and supervisory practices, and satisfaction on recruitment. However, the study did not attempt to investigate whether higher job satisfaction also meant higher adjustment to work. This may be a limitation on the results on this aspect of the investigation.

Socio-Personal Factors

Another hypothesis was that the social characteristics and personal attributes of employees would influence their ability to make adjustment to work. It was contended that education, income, and size of the family of a respondent were the primary influences on his ability to make adjustment to work followed by his background, migratory status, and past employment experience. The study brought out a linear relationship between an employee's adjustment to work and his education, income, and skill. Higher income, higher education, and higher skill of respondents were associated with their superior adjustment to work. The immigrants displayed higher adjustment to work than the local employees, irrespective of job status and factory type. On the whole, it was found that education, income, and migratory status of employees were the major personal attributes that influenced the employee's adjustment to work.

However, it must be mentioned that employees' adjustment to work is not rooted in any one factor. Rather, it is sustained by a set of complex interactions and inter-relationship among work situation, job aspects, and personal attributes. The study brings out that human adjustment to the factory system is influenced by three sets of forces, *viz.*, institutional, job, and socio-personal, operating simultaneously on the work situation. Superior technology, larger size of enterprise, higher job status of employees, higher level of wages, adequate housing, job security, opportuniy for advancement, higher level of education, and income of employees and their migratory status have been found to be the major factors that lead to a greater human adjustment to the factory system. Stated differently, a better adjusted employee is one who works in a superior technology production process of a large size plant, is better educated, earns well, has been provided with living accommodation, perceives that he has opportunities for advancement and will not be thrown out of employment, and is an immigrant.

In addition to the analysis of the human adjustment to the factory system, the study throws light on a number of other aspects of the process of industrialization of the type as characterized by Kota. A few important aspects are described below.

Social Selectivity

It was found that the factory system at Kota was socially selective. The factory workforce was of superior social quality as compared to the general workforce of both Kota and Rajasthan. Compared to the latter, the factory workforce was young in age, more literate, better educated, skilled, earned more, and had less family dependency load.

Cultural Inadequacy

The data reveal that the factory system at Kota attracted a large number of persons from outside Kota who found their traditional culture inadequate. Nearly three-fourths of the factory workforce did not belong to the resident local community. Over two-fifths of the workforce were Harijans (the lowest caste), 90 per cent of them being immigrants. The majority of the workforce came from family occupations that were marginal to the traditional rural economy. Being socially downtrodden and economically uninvolved in the traditional set-up, these groups moved out in search of a new future.

Two Push Factors

Education and youthfulness are the forces that appear to give confidence to people to move out of the traditional set-up and thereby tend to disorganize the traditional society. The majority of the immigrants in the factory workforce were both young and educated.

Emerging Ethos

The study revealed that exposure to industrial employment at Kota influenced workers' perceptions of and attitude towards factory jobs and gave them a greater confidence in their ability to stay in factory employment. Most employees took up factory jobs at Kota not from any particular choice. They learnt of employment opportunities at Kota mostly through friends and relatives and secured jobs through contacts and recommendations. At the time of the investigation most respondents showed definite preference for factory jobs, could identify the formal mechanisms that existed for securing a job, put premium on skill and training for securing employment, and were confident that they needed no external help to find a job, if the current one was lost. Further, the change in perceptions and attitudes was greater in the case of persons employed in factories that had developed formal pay scales, fringe benefits, job security, and training programmes. We find that the factory system initiates changes in the attitudes and values of its workforce, and that once the process of industrialization has started, the necessary ethos emerge along with it.

It was also found that workers attached the greatest importance to wages, and in general were dissatisfied with it. However, they did distinguish good wages from wages. Those employed in factories that paid relatively higher wages were less dissatisfied with their jobs. Finally, the study throws light on the basis of job selection by employees. In selecting a job, it was found, the employee first considered the wages offered to him. Thereafter, he looked for housing facilities and job security in private enterprises, and for promotion opportunities in public undertakings. The employees gave a measure of importance to their work group, and were generally indifferent to working conditions and supervisory practices.

The Implications

The New Worker

The findings of the study enable us to draw a profile of the new worker—as found at Kota. The new worker is a first generation worker. He is a person young in age, who is married, and has a family smaller in size than the average for the region or the country. He is an immigrant from the rural areas of Rajasthan or another part of the country and belongs to the lower castes. In his ancestral home his family does not own land, but is engaged in farming as agricultural labour. He is literate and went to school for four to eight years. The current job is his first experience of organized employment, of supervision and discipline, and of receiving wages at stated intervals. The work history and migration records do not give much information about his motives in opting for factory employment and migrating to a new growth centre, but it is obvious that he found the traditional culture inadequate. The lower social status ascribed to him in the traditional set-up, his peripheral economic interest in agriculture and the marginal existence were strong disincentives to satisfaction with the *status quo*. With the acquisition of a measure of education, he acquired confidence in his ability to seek better prospects elsewhere. His choice to migrate to Kota seemed to have been guided by two considerations. First, a new growth centre, such as Kota, had a much greater potential for employment, could accommodate people with varying skill differentials, and offered less job competition. Second, there were 'friends and relatives' at Kota who acted as vacancy informants, helped in getting a job and in tiding over several problems that could arise out of migration to a new place, adaptation to a new way of life, and during unemployment. The new worker took up the factory job for no reason other than that of making a living.

However, having taken a factory job and having lived in Kota for a few years, a change has taken place in his value-orientation. He has a definite preference for the factory employment, though not for any particular employer or industry or area. He has also developed a priority scale of expectations in the job. He wants good wages, housing facilities, job security, and opportunities for advancement, in the order stated. He has begun to realize that in order to improve his prospects, he should acquire better skills and training. He has come to believe that if he possessed appropriate skills, he would have neither the fear of unemployment, nor the need of help from friends and relatives in getting the future jobs. He thinks that industry values skilled and trained personnel and provides a structured mechanism for the recruitment of operatives of the required kind.

The profile of the new worker, as given above, reinforces three of our statements made in the preceding chapters. First, the process of industrialization generates, apart from material goods and services, an ethos that is necessary for its sustenance. Second, education is a strong force that tends to disorganize the traditional culture and value system. Third, the employees' favourable attitudes to the achievement variables of education, training, and performance provide the necessary basis for improving human efficiency and organizational effectiveness. The industry can play an effective role in making a productive use of this 'favourable' attitude, and in contributing to the further development of human resources.

Job Market

The job market of Kota offered great employment potential (both in reality and as perceived by workers). This is an expected attribute of a growth centre. For a considerable period of time, new industries continue coming in and existing ones expand and diversify production. The demand for labour continues to mount. Having reached the peak, it tapers off, and then begins to decline gradually. A larger number of manual workers employed in plant construction and fabrication are rendered jobless. Many more may become surplus as a result of rationalization of work methods and routinization of production. During its earlier stages, the growth centre attracts, primarily, the unemployed and the under-employed and later, the employed. The changing equilibrium between the demand and the supply of labour, as well as the changes in the nature of demand, has several implications for both the industry and the workers. Unless it can be assumed that the majority of the workforce will move out of the local job market (the evidence is to the contrary), widespread unemployment is bound to take place. The current climate of labour's confidence in job retention, and its favourable attitude to industrial occupations are likely to give place to despondency and frustration. Wage-cutting, industrial conflicts, or excessive pay-rolls could be some of the other consequences. Since the demand for skilled hands is more likely to continue, the industry and the public authorities should pay greater attention to training and skill-generation at this stage of the growth of the region. This will also ease the pressure on industry to import skilled hands who are likely to be already in employment and less willing to move from the metropolis areas to the new growth centres.

Apart from the increased pressure on housing and other civic amenities, and the cost of living at Kota, the job market exercised very little influence on the local community. The latter contributed the bulk of the clerks who showed lower levels of adjustment to work and expressed dissatisfaction with their jobs. The relatively higher living standards of the factory workforce, who were mostly immigrants, and their superior social quality due to the selective recruitment policies of enterprises, were likely to give them a dominant position in local affairs. We are familiar with social tensions and conflicts of the kind in other growth centres. Therefore, policy level efforts need to be made to involve the resident local community in the growth process of the areas.

The high rate of the workers' movement into the job market and inter-plant mobility within the local area have been found to be the other notable features of the Kota job market. A common explanation for the workers' shift from jobs, industries, and regions is that the movement is a function of the differential net advantage and that employees will move from positions of low return to those offering greater rewards. The findings of this study do not contradict the theory but impose certain qualifications on it. One of the most important qualifications is the *will* to shift. The study brings out that despite superior wages and better working conditions, the factories could not attract personnel from the local community. On the other hand, a large number of immigrants from far away places found work in 'Private B' type factories, some of which provided earnings and working conditions that were no better than those on the farms. Again, decisions to change jobs may also depend on the varying circumstances in which workers find themselves. Even when current job conditions provide sufficient disincentive to stay on, workers might not move unless there are opportunities to do so. Finally, the difference in wage rates must be significant so as to offset other considerations that might hold a worker to his present job. All these arguments point to the fact that wage differentials, even where significant, may not necessarily lead to labour mobility. A widening of wage differentials may result in a higher wage bill for a firm without attracting more people to the pay-roll. The study supports the theory that wages remain the most important consideration in job selection by employees. But wages may generate job shifts when coupled with other things, such as job security and housing in private enterprises, and promotion opportunities in public undertakings.

Trade Unionism

It might be pointed out that the study missed an important aspect of the factory system, namely the trade union situation. The omission was not deliberate. Kota industries did not have any unions functioning during the period of the conception and fieldwork of the study. The pilot study (March-April 1964) did reveal the existence of two unions that were registered with the government. But they were neither organizing bodies nor bargaining agents. Both were more akin to an attorney's office which rendered legal advice in return for fees. The railway workshop ('Public A') was unionized but the union was a part of the national complex of the railwaymen's unions. It neither contributed to the development of unions in the local area nor drew anything from it. Therefore, issues relating to unionism could be considered in the private enterprises only. No data on the subject were available to us, either published or from primary sources. As such all we had to go by was our impressions gathered during our stay at Kota, discussions with several knowledgeable persons, and by the experience of other growth centres. We anticipate the labour movement in Kota to develop in stages. The chemical plants ('Private A') and scores of small enterprises ('Private B') will be organized on local issues, and a number of factory level unions will come into existence. (This had already happened by April 1967.) However, these unions will tend to be *ad hoc* bodies in character, and unstable in structure. They will be given to agitation and noise, and are likely to be less competent either to negotiate across the table or to enforce discipline amongst their members. In its second stage, most of these factory level unions will move towards general industrial unionism. The bargaining processes are likely to shift from the plant unions to the general unions. The outside leaders drawn mostly from political parties will assume more crucial positions in the unions. If a firm is to look for a responsible and rational bargaining agent, then the political colour of unions is less relevant than their authority with workers. We expect that the industrial unions will be more responsible and rational than the factory unions. They will also be more hard-hitting and tough bargainers. In any case the companies should develop knowledge, skills, and competency in the managerial group to meet the new kind of union-force.

Management Policies

The industry has a vital role to play in the development of a workforce which is stable, efficient, productive and disciplined. The process of transformation of rural labour into an industrial workforce is complex, full of strains and stresses. The industry could develop policies and adopt measures to help the new entrants to the factory job market in making the necessary adjustment to work without undergoing the avoidable stressful experiences. Even though the informal sources of vacancy information and of getting jobs are likely to continue, the formal mechanisms for the purpose need to be developed and popularized. The latter are likely to assume greater importance in view of the longer exposure of workers to factory employment and the increase in the demand for skilled operatives. More effective functioning of the public employment exchanges in the area would also help. The importance of training for all types of employees has already been discussed at two different places in the study, and needs no further emphasis.

A very significant factor in enhancing the employees' commitment to the industrial way of life is their perception of the security afforded to them by the factory system. The basic security against unemployment and the resultant loss in earnings and against illness and incapacity, was provided by the joint family. The need for social intercourse and emotional security were met within the caste group and the village community. Unless the factory system is able to provide alternative systems to meet these needs in the new environment, the workers are more likely to continue keeping their ties with the traditional system. This will hinder their adjustment to work in industrial occupations. In the absence of substitute mechanisms in the factory system, it might even be desirable for workers to keep alive their associations with the traditional system. At least, they will feel secure as long as they stay in the factory job market. It is, therefore, imperative for the factory system to develop substitute security-needs' meeting mechanisms. Certain legislative measures such as the Employees' State Insurance Scheme, the Employees' Provident Fund Scheme, the health and welfare provisions in the Factories Act, 1948, etc., are a step in the right direction. They deserve unqualified support from the industry and proper enforcement by the government machinery. Job security, minimum wages, and incremental time scales of pay are other measures that would contribute to higher adjustment to work. The findings of the study sufficiently bear out this fact. Finally, policies need to be developed to cushion the shock to workers of occupational, regional and social mobility. Housing is one of the most important needs of workers. The rate of building activity in the township has lagged far behind the rate of immigration. The workers consider housing next to wages in order of importance. The factories would do well to undertake company housing programmes.

Industrialization is the key to economic development. It is also the process of acculturation. It influences the forms of social structure, value systems, motivations and norms and in turn is influenced by them. Strategies of change and growth, and of influencing human behaviour, call for simultaneous action on a number of fronts. Material progress is impossible to achieve without concomitant changes in social structure, values, and motivations. The desired nature and pace of change cannot be achieved in the absence of appropriate incentives and rewards. The process of industrialization at Kota provides us with insights into the problems of human adjustment and of growth and change, and tells us about the forces that need to be generated, or those to be harnessed, in achieving the national objectives.

APPENDIX-A

A STUDY OF THE EMPLOYEES' ADJUSTMENT TO FACTORY SYSTEM

A. *Identification*:

		Code
1.	Name	
2.	Job Status	1 2 3
3.	Name of the Company	
4.	Department	1 2 3 4 5
5.	Ticket No.	
6.	Migratory Status	1 2 3

Schedule A

B. *Personal Particulars*:

Question	Answer	Code
1. Age:		1 2 3 4 5
2. Religion:		1 2 3 4 5
3. (a) Sub-caste:		1 2 3 4
(b) Caste:		
4. Marital Status:		1 2 3
5. Education:		1 2 3 4 5
6. Technical Training:		1 2 3 4 5
7. (a) Native Place:		1 2 3
(b) Approximate Population:		1 2
(c) District:		1 2 3
8. Occupation:		
(a) Father:		
(b) Grandfather:		
9. Length of Service in the Present Job:	Year Month	1 2 3 4 5 6
10. (a) Total Monthly Family Income:	Rs.	1 2 3 4
(b) Gross Monthly Wages:	Rs.	1 2 3 4
(c) Total Take Home Pay Per Month:	Rs.	1 2 3 4
(d) Amount Remitted Home:	Rs.	1 2 3 4

APPENDIX-A

C. (*a*) *Family Particulars*:

Sl. No.	Rela- tionship	Education	Economic status	Occu- pation	Month- ly earnings of earner	If living along with since when	Misc.
I	II	III	IV	V	VI	VII	VIII
1.							
2.							
3.							
4.							
5.							

(*b*) Total number of earners in the family:
(*c*) Total monthly income of the family:
(*d*) Total number of dependents:

D. *Previous Employment*:

Sl. No.	Company/ Employer	Place of work	Occu- pation	Salary	Age	Number of depen- dents	Period From	Period To	Reasons for leaving the job
I	II	III	IV	V	VI	VII	VIII	IX	X

E. *Current Employment*:

Give particulars of the current employment, from the date of joining till to-date.

Sl. No.	Period From	Period To	Designation	Total wages	Reasons for change
I	II	III	IV	V	VI
1.					
2.					
3.					
4.					
5.					

F. *Unemployment Particulars*:

Sl. No.	Period From	Period To	Place where resided	Persons with whom resided	Source of livelihood	Misc.
I	II	III	IV	V	VI	VII

APPENDIX-A

G. Job Market:

Question	Answer	Code
I. Questions for Immigrants only		
1. When did you first come to Kota?		
2. What were your considerations for coming to Kota?		
3. When you first came to Kota, for how long did you plan to stay?		
4. How did you come to know about the employment opportunities at Kota?		
5. What prompted you to choose current work?		
II. Questions for all		
6. If your present job is over, will you look for another job?	Yes/No	
7. If yes, give		
(*i*) Place of work:		
(*ii*) Nature of work:		
8. How will you try for getting another job?		
9. How long will it take?		
10. What counts most in getting a job these days?		
11. Name the job that you desire most to have with the present employer?		
12. (*i*) Do you think you can get that job?	Yes/No	
(*ii*) If yes, how long will it take?		
(*iii*) What are your salary expectations at the desired job?		
13. What is needed most in getting promotion in your company?		
14. (*i*) If you are lucky enough to come by Rs. 5,000 in cash, would you leave the present job?	Yes/No	

Question	Answer	Code
(ii) If yes, what will you do after leaving the job?		
(iii) If no, what will you do with this money?		
15. (i) If it were possible, how much education would you have wanted?		
(ii) With what aim would you have wanted such education?		
16. How much education would you like a son of yours to have?		
17. (i) Would you like to go for training for getting promotion in future?	Yes/No	
(ii) If yes, mention		
(a) Type of training:		
(b) Place of training:		

Schedule B

Question	Answer	Code
1. Can you hold your job as long as you wish?		
2. Can a similar job elsewhere in Kota get you wages more than what you earn currently?		
3. Is your company interested in helping you to improve skills?		
4. Does your company promote only such persons who prove their abilities?		
5. Will you be promoted if you could improve your skills?		
6. Does your company care for suggestions to improve work methods?		
7. If you were to stay with the current company till the age of 65, would you be able to save for your old age?		

APPENDIX-A

Question	Answer	Code
8. Are your grievances given a proper hearing?		
9. Is your work-place clean and hygienic?		
10. Do you think your work is tiring?		
11. Are you given clear and specific job instructions?		
12. Are you supplied tools and other materials promptly?		
13. Is the company interested in seeing you properly housed?		
14. Do you have to work with people you don't like?		
15. Will the company help you in a personal/family problem?		
16. Does your company care for you?		
17. On balance, is your company better than most others in Kota?		
18. Do you think that you have chosen an appropriate occupation for yourself?		
19. Is your work interesting?		
20. Will you leave this company if a job similar to the current one is available elsewhere at Kota?		
21. Will you advise your friends to join/serve your company?		
22. If it were possible for you to start all over again, will you choose the same occupation?		

23. Generally, most persons consider several aspects of a job before accepting it. We like to know what your job expectations are. Listed below are nine job aspects. First, select three which you consider as most important, then select three which are least important. Finally place all nine in a rank order.

Sl. No.	Job aspect	Most important	Important	Least important	Rank
1.	Promotion opportunities				
2.	Job security				
3.	Housing				
4.	Wages				
5.	Working conditions				
6.	Co-workers				
7.	Bonus				
8.	Supervisors				
9.	Welfare services				

24. Please place the following nine aspects of your job in the rank order, from the best to the worst. Follow the procedure given below :

Sl. No	Job aspect	Very Good	Good	Bad	Rank
1.	Welfare services				
2.	Co-workers				
3.	Wages				
4.	Job security				
5.	Supervisors				
6.	Promotion opportunities				
7.	Working conditions				
8.	Housing				
9.	Bonus				

APPENDIX-A

25. Do you want to add anything more to what you have already said?

   ....
   ....

26. Interviewer's assessment of the respondent's comprehension of questions and cooperation:

   ....
   ....

27. Interviewer's other remarks:

   ....
   ....

DATE :   **INTERVIEWER**

Results of the test of independence of the items in the job attitude scale

(SCHEDULE B)

Item Nos. on Schedule B	X^2 (Chi square)	Level of significance*	Remarks
1.	18·74	·001	Significant
2.	0·01	·05	Insignificant
3.	48·41	·001	Significant
4.	22·51	·001	Significant
5.	45·73	·001	Significant
6.	41·69	·001	Significant
7.	1·35	·05	Insignificant
8.	45·39	·001	Significant
9.	25·27	·001	Significant
10.	37·60	·001	Significant
11.	14·16	·001	Significant
12.	0·001	·05	Insignificant
13.	12·87	·001	Significant
14.	0·05	·05	Insignificant
15.	15·75	·001	Significant
16.	58·51	·001	Significant
17.	29·18	·001	Significant
18.	16·57	·001	Significant
19.	6·91	·01	Significant
20.	12·22	·001	Significant
21.	4·66	·05	Significant
22.	16·86	·001	Significant

*df=one in every case.

Appendix—B

THE CONSTRUCTION WORKER

THIS study of the workforce in the construction industry was carried out at Kota at the work-sites and the surrounding areas of the Chambal Valley Project. The purpose of the study* was

*The study is based on 450 interviews with respondents employed by eleven construction companies, and the Irrigation and the Public Works Departments, and working at Kota during April-July, 1964. The interviews were conducted with the help of a specially designed questionnaire, and were held mostly at work-sites. Direct observation and interviews with contractors, government officers concerned with labour administration, and union leaders proved helpful in understanding the organization and the operations of the industry. A team of four interviewers lived at Kota for over six months, established rapport with workers, and mixed freely with them. This enabled us to overcome the difficulties created by the limited cooperation offered by the contractors and the respondents' fear of contractors in talking to us.

The field work for the study commenced in April 1964. Our preliminary enquiries with the local Employment Exchanges revealed that all the construction labour at Kota was employed through construction companies, contractors, and the government departments of Irrigation and Public Works. The employment position was as below:

Employing agencies	No.	No. of persons employed
1. Construction companies	60	16,500
2. Contractors	15	500
3. Public Works Department and Irrigation Department	—	3,000
Total:		20,000

This information was checked with the local officers including the Inspector of Factories, the Assistant Director of Industries, and the Minimum Wages Inspector. They were generally in agreement with the figures.

The next step was to locate these companies, and to meet their officers. As a result of our discussion with the persons concerned, the criteria to select the employing agencies for purposes of this study were evolved. It was decided that in order to qualify to be on our sample, an agency should to undertake a field survey with a view:

(i) to understanding the work organization, the operations, and the characteristics of the construction industry;
(ii) to ascertaining the social and demographic characteristics of the workforce;
(iii) to understanding the nature and the pattern of workers' mobility, and the factors influencing it; and
(iv) to assessing the extent to which the experience of work in construction industry developed the potentialities of workers to grow into a 'stable' industrial workforce.

The Chambal Valley Projects Scheme envisaged harnessing the river Chambal by constructing three dams across it so as to

---

meet all the four requirements listed below:

(i) It should be on the 'Approved List' of the government. (This implied that the selected agencies were committed to provide the basic norms of safety, health, welfare, working conditions, and minimum wages to their employees.)
(ii) It should employ, at the time of the survey, at least 300 workers, and should have employed not less than 100 workers during the preceding six months. (The minimum strength of labour employed was considered necessary for structuring personnel policies.)
(iii) The headquarters of the agency should be at Kota.
(iv) It should have the major portion of its work-sites in or around Kota. (Some agencies which were engaged on work at places far away from Kota set up their own shanty towns for workers, and colonies for officers, and the employees had no contacts with the mainstream of life at Kota. We were interested in those agencies whose employees got opportunities of exposure to city life, manufacturing industries, and a diverse group of workers.)

Considered on the basis of these criteria, only 11 of the 60 construction companies, and the two government departments qualified for the study. They employed a total of 5,408 workmen, which constituted the universe for the study.

Further, the universe consisted of workers, supervisors called mistris, and clerks called munshis. The three groups displayed basic differences in terms of the degree and the nature of skill possessed, wage rates, task assignment, and management's perception of their (groups) importance. Therefore, the universe was stratified according to the job status of its constituents. Each stratum in the sample constituted 8·33 per cent of its respective universe. The representative proportions in the universe were maintained within the sample also.

utilize its water for purposes of irrigation and generation of electricity. The work on the two of the three dams, namely *Gandhi Sagar* and the *Kota Barrage*, started in 1958, and with their completion in 1960-61, the first phase of the scheme was over. Following the availability of power, and facilitated by liberal industrial and fiscal policies of the State government, new industries started coming up and grew rapidly. The construction of dams, canals, power houses, and a large number of factories attracted a large number of workers to Kota. In 1959, the average daily employment in construction industry at Kota was 6,868. In April 1964, it stood at 20,000. The construction companies were contracting agencies which secured assignments from either the Chambal Project authorities or the industrial enterprises, or from both. The eleven companies from where the respondents were drawn were large firms that specialized in construction work, and held contracts in different parts of the country. Also, they were non-Rajasthani enterprises. Of the remaining 49 companies, only eight were local firms. The 15 contractors were sub-agents of some of the larger companies, and held no direct assignments from the Project authorities.

The operations involved in carrying out assignments in this industry, as obtaining at Kota, were as follows:

(*i*) earthwork, stone breaking and crushing at the work-site;
(*ii*) making of buildings, bridges, roads, dams, canals, power houses;
(*iii*) erection of plant buildings, and work ancillary to or connected with plant fabrication, and installation of machinery;
(*iv*) operating vehicles and cranes engaged in transhipment of material at work-site, and maintenance of such vehicles; and
(*v*) masonry, carpentry, blacksmithy, welding, mechanical jobs, etc.

All the above stated operations were carried out by workers under the supervision of engineers and other senior level technical personnel. The operatives were classified into skilled, semi-skilled, and unskilled categories according to the nature of work performed by them as below:

Skilled: Masons, carpenters, blacksmiths, stone cutters, mechanics, drivers, etc. (These personnel were called mistris if they reported directly to the engineers. In addition, this category also included clerks called munshis.)

Semi-skilled All categories of workers as stated in the 'skilled' category, if they were working under and reported to a mistri.

Unskilled: Workers engaged on earth work, stone breaking and crushing, digging, transhipment, load carrying, and similar work. (These personnel were designated as jamadars, beldars, bandhanis, watchmen, water carriers, etc.)

The Characteristics of the Industry

The construction industry is both unique and distinct from other industries in several respects. First, in order to secure work a company has to be on the Approved List of Contractors maintained by the government. Being 'approved' testifies to the financial stability of a firm, to its ability to execute work successfully up to a certain level, and to its capacity to honour the obligations towards its workers as specified under the Central Public Works Department Rules. After securing the 'contract', a company recruits labour and starts work. In the normal course, workers are paid advances and, later on, wages at short frequencies. But the companies get 'payment' for the work executed only at long intervals. This involves considerable financial outlay. As work is executed mostly either at the 'Standard Rates' or at a small percentage variation, only large-scale operations would yield sizable profits. Therefore, the companies try to obtain bigger contracts, where execution is possible only by a large labour force always available at call. A construction company having adequate capital and technical know-how might not succeed unless it has the ability to command the services of a sizable unskilled labour force.

Second, labour intensiveness is particularly peculiar to this industry. In order to make a mistri (skilled person) productive, a gang of about ten unskilled workers is supplied to him. On the other hand, having employed ten unskilled persons, a company must have a mistri to make them give their money's worth. As skilled labour is in short supply, the companies can hire them only at competitive rates. This pressure on the wage bill can be offset if the company has access to the vast supply of unskilled agricultural labour in the hinterland—scarcity-hit and poor districts all over the country—who could be hired at cheaper rates. Thus, an ongoing company must establish contacts in the interior districts for its labour supply, and continuously look for cheap labour. It cannot avoid paying much higher wages to skilled workers, so it must work to keep the wages of unskilled workers as low as possible.

Third, construction work is essentially a 'contract' job. The tenure of employment is purely temporary, and no one can view his job beyond the contract period. There are constant changes in the workplace and of employers for most workers. Work is performed at the work-site. Everyone moves away immediately after the task is over. Of necessity, the nature of operations is seasonal. Work on buildings, roads, quarries, dams, etc., cannot be performed during monsoons for obvious reasons. Fourth, time-rate wages are the exception, and are given only to a few mistris, munshis, and highly-skilled personnel. Most of the workers are paid piece-rates based on their output. Compensation for work is always in cash, and no perquisites or overhead benefits are available to anyone. Fifth, this is one of those sectors of industrial activity where labour laws pertaining to hours and conditions of work, safety, health, welfare, etc., are conspicuous by their absence. Provisions have been laid down through executive orders, but are difficult to enforce and implement. Sixth, the work is performed generally in gangs. Employees work in groups; work measurement and payment is made on group basis only. Finally, due to the unskilled nature of work, the piece-rate system of payment and the absence of protective legislation, workers encourage their womenfolk and children to work to help to increase output. They consider their work as a family assignment.

Because of these inherent characteristics of the industry, it is obvious that the work is so temporary, unorganized, and seasonal that it hardly permits stabilization of employer-employee relationships. Methods of pay compensation, gang work, and absence of protective legislation create conditions in which it is possible for the high-skill workers to obtain exceptionally high rates of wages. Seasonal work, the temporary nature of employment, and low wages make it necessary for the workers to maintain their land and village ties and return to the same when necessary. Thus, though construction is an industry in usage and in legal parlance, yet it is a different kind of industry.

The Work Organization

The line hierarchy of a construction company is as shown below.

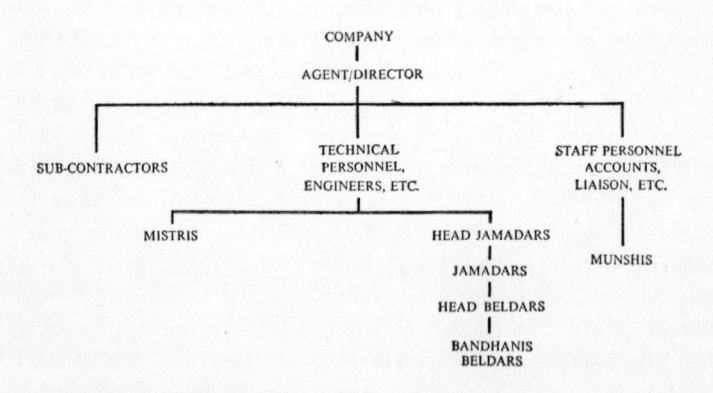

```
                    COMPANY
                       |
                 AGENT/DIRECTOR
     ┌─────────────────┼─────────────────┐
                   TECHNICAL
SUB-CONTRACTORS   PERSONNEL,        STAFF PERSONNEL
                  ENGINEERS, ETC.   ACCOUNTS,
                                    LIAISON, ETC.
     ┌──────────────────┐                │
   MISTRIS           HEAD JAMADARS    MUNSHIS
                         |
                      JAMADARS
                         |
                    HEAD BELDARS
                         |
                     BANDHANIS
                      BELDARS
```

The constituents of a work-group at the construction site are as follows:

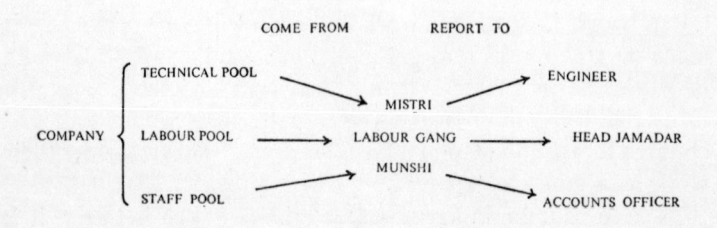

```
                    COME FROM        REPORT TO
         ┌ TECHNICAL POOL ─────┐
         │                     ↘         ↗ ENGINEER
         │                     MISTRI
COMPANY ─┤ LABOUR POOL ────→ LABOUR GANG ────→ HEAD JAMADAR
         │                     ↗
         │                   MUNSHI
         └ STAFF POOL ────────┘        ↘ ACCOUNTS OFFICER
```

A construction company may have work going on at more than one site in a particular area. Every work-site has a head jamadar to supply the unskilled labour required. At a particular work-site, the company engineer will lay down the quantum, the nature, and the manner of work. He will assign some mistris to do the jobs, and ask the head jamadar to furnish the required number of labour gangs, but does no hiring, firing, or transfer. He is only a work supervisor. Thus, the work relationship is different from the reporting relationship. Mistris report to engineers. Beldars and jamadars report to head jamadars, who in turn report to the engineer. Munshis report to staff officers. In order to constitute a work group, the engineers assign work to mistris, the head jamadars depute labour gangs to work with mistris, and the staff departments send over munshis for record keeping, etc. The mistri remains the work supervisor, but the head jamadar remains the administrative head for the labour. A munshi is a staff help to the unit. In practice, the head jamadar becomes the most senior officer on the work-site. He controls labour. Long experience on the job has given him enough knowledge about mistris' skills. He earns more than anyone else. The company values him more because of his control over labour. In case of a clash with his supervisor, he is more likely to be favoured by the company.

A beldar is generally an unskilled worker. A number of beldars constitute a gang. The gang leader is called head beldar, and he in addition to working himself is also entrusted with the task of ensuring the required output by his gang and getting it measured. A number of gangs work under the supervision of a jamadar. The jamadar himself is a worker, and is also responsible for recruitment, ensuring output standards at the work-site, participating in work measurement on behalf of his workers, taking attendance, and assisting in payment of wages. The head jamadar is one of the most crucial officials in the set-up. A company must have at least as many head jamadars as the number of work-sites under its operation. The head jamadar supervises the jamadars' work and serves as the link between the management and the gangs. The mistri is a skilled person who is assigned a gang to work with. The munshi is a clerk responsible for time-keeping, calculation of payments, and other clerical tasks.

The Work Performance

As observed earlier, construction work is essentially temporary, outdoor, unskilled, and piece-rate. Standards for working hours and working conditions do exist, but are difficult to enforce and implement. At Kota, workers generally lived in make-shift hutments put up near their workplaces. Those employed on earth work generally adjusted their working hours according to the season. In summer, unless continuous shifts were worked, most of the workers employed on earth work worked from 5 to 11 a.m., and from 4 to 8 p.m. It was generally observed that workers were also helped by the members of their families. The entire family was at the work-site—women worked along with men, young children looked after infants. Contrary to the provisions of the rules, workers had to make their own arrangements for drinking water, washing, toilet facilities, etc. In the course of interviews, workers expressed indifference to the work organization, their working hours and working conditions. Family employment, irregular and long working hours that mostly varied with the seasons, and the absence of regulation of working conditions, as experienced by construction workers were no different from agricultural employment. At any rate, they were returning home after the contract was over. So, why bother about anything other than earning as much as possible?

The Wage Rates

In accordance with the provisions of the Minimum Wages Act, 1948, the State government has fixed minimum rates of wages for workers engaged by it on road construction, building operations, and stone breaking and crushing. The necessary staff to enforce these rates in respect of workers employed directly by it has been appointed. As regards workers engaged through contractors, a 'fair wage' clause has been provided in the Contract of Agreement that is required to be signed by every contractor before he is given any job. In case of any contravention, the contract is liable to be cancelled. In respect of private contractors, there is no authority to enforce the fixed minimum rates. A worker may, however, lodge a complaint against the contractor paying wages less than the minimum. In practice, such complaints could be made only at the risk of losing the job. The consolidated wages fixed by the State government for certain categories of workers are given in Tables 1 and 2.

TABLE 1

Table showing occupational time-rates of workers engaged through contractors in building and construction industry at Kota as fixed under the Minimum Wages Act, 1948

Category of workers	Wages per day Minimum (Rs.)	Maximum (Rs.)
Mason	3·50	7·50
Carpenter	4·00	6·00
Blacksmith	3·00	7·00
Stone Cutter	2·50	3·00
Fitter	3·00	6·00
Driller	2·00	3·00
Mechanic	3·50	4·00
Driver	150·00 p.m.	
Mate	80·00 p.m.	
Mistri	125·00 to	180·00 p.m.
Watchman	30·00 to	60·00 p.m.
Water Carrier	2·50	3·00
Mazdoor	1·50	2·00
Mazdoor Woman	1·25	1·50

TABLE 2

Table showing piece-rates for jobs done by workers employed through contractors in building and construction industry at Kota as fixed under the Minimum Wages Act, 1948

Category of work	Unit	Rate of payment
Masonry	100 c.ft.	Rs. 13·00 to 13·50
Concreting	1000 c.ft.	Rs. 12·00
Carpentry	1 sq.ft.	Rs. 0·75
Earth Work	1000 c.ft.	Rs. 11·20 to 15·00
Stone Breaking	100 c.ft.	Rs. 20·00

The Recruitment

The principal concern of a construction company is to obtain contracts for jobs, and to execute them. In order to discharge its obligations successfully, a company must either retain a sizable workforce or have it available at call. However, at a point of time, the employer can provide work only for a short duration, but he wants workers to commit themselves to work for him whenever required without having obtained any assurance on continued employment or wage rates. Ideally, an employer would like to tell his workers, 'You work for the duration of the present contract. If I get another contract you will be transferred there; otherwise you go away. But when I need you again, you must come back and work for me.'

JAMADARS

The hiring practices that meet just those employees' objectives have been developed through the institution of the *jamadari* and the *peshgi* systems. Jamadars are responsible for hiring labour, retaining them during the contract period, and bringing them back when the company has a new contract. The jamadar uses the *peshgi* for this purpose. The *peshgi* means a money advance given to workers at the time of recruitment. A worker pledges his labour in return for the *peshgi*. The contractor furnishes this money to his jamadars, and the latter advance it to workers, and are held personally responsible for its recovery. In return, the rewards of a jamadar comprise monthly retainer, commission from the employer on the basis of persons employed through him every day and a further commission from the workers for whom he has found work. He is a guarantor of the employer's money, of the workers' employment, and a continued link between the two.

However, the *jamadari* system encourages recruitment based on caste and village ties. If a jamadar has to stand guarantee for money advanced to workers, it will be logical for him to look for workers who can be relied upon. It is natural that persons considered reliable by him are often his relatives, friends, men of his own caste or village, on whom social and communal pressure can be exerted in case of default. It is not uncommon to identify work-sites by the caste or the place of origin of the labour force working there.

A jamadar may keep working for his contractors/company even after the assignment is over. The continuity of association between the two is facilitated by the varying amounts of *peshgi* that remain unreturned, and for which the jamadar stood guarantee. The unreturned *peshgi* keeps workers available at the call of contractors, gives workers the hope of a possible future employment, obliges the latter to provide work, and maintains the *jamadari* link between the two. The *peshgi* system has become institutionalized over the years. It is a symbol of having been initiated to the work group and the gang. It is evidence of a person's creditworthiness, of dependability, and of enjoying the confidence of the jamadar. Workers expect *peshgi*, and insist on receiving it as an interest-free credit against future work, and use it to pay back debts from village moneylenders, to meet their social obligations, to build a house, or to buy land, cattle, etc. Everyone understands that *peshgi* has to be returned, but no one is keen that it be paid back in full.

While the amount varied, a jamadar usually got a monthly salary of Rs. 100 and a commission of five paise per man-shift worked through him. In addition, he charged five paise per day from every worker for whom he found work. The *peshgi* given to workers varied considerably, and depended on the latter's reputation. It was found more common for a contractor to give a *peshgi* of Rs. 500 to a person who was considered good, dependable, and was expected to work for six months. A new worker might receive anything from Rs. 50 to 100. Persons who came to the work-site on their own, and were not known to a jamadar, got no *peshgi* in the beginning, and were looked down upon by others. A new worker would like to work his way up to receive *peshgi*. The amounts of unreturned *peshgi* varied with different jamadars and were not disclosed. However, our estimate is that a jamadar who worked a gang of one hundred workers for nearly eighteen months would have about three thousand rupees as unpaid *peshgis* to his account. During the same period, he would have earned—but not paid—the *jamadari* commission of nearly two thousand rupees. Thus, though the total of the *peshgi* given at the time of commencement of work may add up to twenty thousand rupees or so, the eventual risk to the contractor is very small. Unreturned *peshgis* are not a few large sums, but many small ones.

MISTRIS

The recruitment practices and problems relating to mistris are of an entirely different nature. They are skilled workers who can conveniently find jobs in the organized industries. Consequently, the construction companies offer them remuneration that is about twice as high as a person can get in a manufacturing establishment. The companies often resort to vacancy advertisements in newspapers and employment exchanges. However, the principal sources of mistri intake for a company are other companies. The mistris generally change employers in groups. Persons belonging to the same area, or those who previously worked in the same company, may form a craft group and decide to stay together. If a company can negotiate terms and attract one person, the rest of the group may also follow him. In fact, if a group is interested in shifting over, premium terms are arranged. In the course of interviews, many contractors displayed ambivalent feelings towards the craft groups amongst mistris. They found it convenient if the personnel could be recruited in groups. But they did not like the terms that had to be given and the subsequent demands that were put forward by mistris on the threat of leaving the company. The employers tried to meet the situation in two ways. They attempted to develop a practice that a company should not recruit mistris who had deserted another company in the same area. The attempt was not successful. Some companies had encouraged their engineers and head jamadars to work with mistris in developing personal loyalties towards them. Quite a few mistris reported that they worked for the company because they liked one of its engineers or head jamadars. Thus, the industry had so far found no satisfactory method of recruitment of mistris.

MUNSHIS

The recruitment of munshis was not considered a problem by any company. A good number of persons were locally available, and could be had by calling at the employment exchange. In fact, the companies offered wages that were not relatively higher than what a matriculate clerk could get elsewhere, and munshi turnover was not high.

THE SOCIAL CHARACTERISTICS OF THE WORKFORCE

In the course of our discussion on the work organization of the construction industry in the previous section, we dealt with the recruitment, the wages, and the work performance of workers such as beldars, head beldars, jamadars, mistris, and munshis. In this section, we report data relating to the several social and demographic characteristics of the respondents as collected in the course of interviews with them. The worker, mistri, and munshi groups have been compared with one another; and wherever possible comparisons have also been made with those in the surrounding areas.

Age

It will be observed from Table 3 that whereas only 11 per cent of respondents were 40 years or more old, 68 per cent were

TABLE 3

Table showing age distribution of respondents by job status

Category		Less than 20 years	20-30 years	30-40 years	Above 40 years	Total
Workers	No.	68	170	68	37	343
	%	19·8	49·6	19·8	10·8	100·0
Mistris	No.	1	21	11	6	39
	%	2·6	53·8	28·2	15·4	100·0
Munshis	No.	12	35	14	7	68
	%	17·6	15·5	20·6	10·3	100·0
Overall	No.	81	226	93	50	450
	%	18·00	50·2	20·7	11·1	100·0

less than 30. The worker and the munshi groups had similar age structures, but mistris were older. Eighty-two per cent of mistris fell in the age group 21-40 against 60·4 per cent for workers, and 72·1 per cent for munshis. On the whole, the sample is characterized by its youthfulness.

Literacy

TABLE 4

Table showing literacy rate of respondents by job status

Category		Illiterate	Literate	Total
Workers	No.	213	130	343
	%	62·1	37·9	100·0
Mistris	No.	2	37	39
	%	5·2	94·8	100·0
Munshis	No.	1	67	68
	%	1·5	98·5	100·0
Overall	No.	216	234	450
	%	48·2	51·8	100·0

For the purpose of this study, a person was considered to be literate if he could write a letter and read a newspaper in any one of the Indian languages. Judged by this criterion, the literacy rate in respect of the respondents was 51·8 per cent. Analyzed by job status, 99 per cent munshis, 95 per cent mistris, and 38 per cent workers were literate. It may be mentioned that according to the 1961 Census, the literacy rate was 43·6 per cent for Kota town, 19·1 per cent for Kota district, 14·7 per cent for Rajasthan, and 23·7 per cent for the country as a whole.

Educational Level

It will be noticed from Table 5 that 79·2 per cent of mistris and 60·3 per cent of munshis were educated up to 'high school and above' against 5·2 per cent of workers in this category.

TABLE 5

Table showing levels of education of respondents by job status

Category		Illiterate (No formal schooling)	Four years of schooling	Below high school	High school and above	Total
Workers	No.	213	75	37	18	343
	%	62·1	21·9	10·8	5·2	100·0
Mistris	No.	2	3	3	31	39
	%	5·2	7·8	7·8	79·2	100·0
Munshis	No.	1	11	15	41	68
	%	1·5	16·1	22·1	60·3	100·0
Overall	No.	216	89	55	90	450
	%	48·2	19·6	12·2	20·0	100·0

Only 5·2 per cent of mistris were illiterate. Relatively, a large percentage of munshis had below high school education. Compared to Kota and Rajasthan, the literacy rate for this group is much higher. It is significant that 16 per cent of workers had 8 to 10 years of schooling. Equally noticeable is the fact that 40 per cent of munshis were not even matriculates, which is generally considered a minimum qualification for clerical jobs.

Skill

All munshis were clerks employed on the basis of proficiency in clerical work. Mistris were high-skilled personnel. Therefore, analysis by skill was done for workers only. They were categorized into skilled, semi-skilled, and unskilled groups according to the classification done by the Public Works Department. Carpenters, masons, blacksmiths, welders, drivers, etc., were considered as skilled workers, their helpers as semi-skilled, and the remaining as unskilled. Of the total workers, 68·5 per cent were unskilled, 30·6 per cent semi-skilled, and 0·9 per cent skilled. However, no worker was classified skilled or semi-skilled by employers in terms of the Minimum Wages Act, 1948.

Origin

The respondents were asked to state the district from which they originated and whether their native place was a village or a town.* It was found that 83·2 per cent of workers, 43·6 per cent of mistris, and 57·4 per cent of munshis came from rural areas. The majority of mistris had urban background, but workers predominantly belonged to rural areas. Table 6 spells out the origin of respondents by their job status.

TABLE 6
Table showing the origin of respondents by job status

Category			Kota	Rajasthan	Other States	Total
Workers	{	No.	71	166	106	343
		%	20·7	48·4	30·6	100·0
Mistris	{	No.	5	8	26	39
		%	12·8	20·5	66·7	100·0
Munshis	{	No.	20	18	30	68
		%	29·4	26·5	44·1	100·0
Overall	{	No.	96	192	162	450
		%	21·3	42·7	36·0	100·0

A perusal of Table 6 brings out that 64 per cent of the total respondents belonged to Rajasthan. An analysis by job status revealed an uneven distribution of Rajasthani respondents in the three respective groups. Only one-third of the mistris belonged to Rajasthan, against two-thirds of the workers in this group. Kota district furnished more munshis than workers, and very few mistris. The majority of workers came from Rajasthan, the majority of mistris from other States, and munshis were evenly divided between Rajasthan and other States.

Religion and Caste

An analysis of respondents by their professed religion revealed that of the total, 88·4 per cent were Hindus, 10·0 per cent Muslims, 1·1 per cent Sikhs, and 0·4 per cent Christians. Muslims

---
*A town is taken here as a place with not less than 5,000 inhabitants.

were equally dispersed among the worker and the mistri groups, but were less among the munshi group. Christians constituted 7·7 per cent of mistris against their overall average of 0·4 in the sample.

Table 7 spells out the caste stratification of Hindu respondents.

TABLE 7

Table showing caste stratification of Hindu respondents by job status

Category		Brahmins	Kshatriyas	Vaishyas	Harijans	Total
Workers	No.	24	86	10	185	305
	%	7·9	28·2	3·3	60·7	100·0
Mistris	No.	8	12	9	3	32
	%	25·0	37·5	28·1	9·4	100·0
Munshis	No.	14	19	19	9	61
	%	22·9	31·1	31·1	14·8	100·0
Overall	No.	46	117	38	197	398
	%	11·5	29·6	9·8	49·7	100·0

The table shows that of the total respondents, half were Harijans. An analysis by job status further revealed that among the worker group, 60·7 per cent were Harijans, 28·2 per cent Kshatriyas, 7·9 per cent Brahmins, and 3·3 per cent Vaishyas. Whereas the majority of workers were Harijans, only a small percentage of mistris belonged to this caste group. Of the munshis, only 14·8 per cent were Harijans, and the remainder was evenly divided among all castes.

Family

Only 69 per cent of the respondents were married, which included 71 per cent of workers, 64 per cent of mistris, and 66 per cent of munshis.

SIZE OF FAMILY

The average size of the family* in respect of the sample worked out at 4·76. Analyzed by job status, the average size of the family in munshis was the largest, followed by workers and mistris in that order, *viz.*, 5·15, 4·95, and 4·19. The average size of the family in respect of our sample was smaller as compared to similar figures for Kota district (4·97) and Rajasthan (5·34).

In fact, it has been found more generally that the immigrants have smaller families than the local residents.**

ECONOMIC STATUS

The economic status of the members within a family is as shown in Table 8.

TABLE 8

Table showing economic status of the members within a family

Category	Average size of family	No. of earners	No. of dependents	E. D. Ratio
Workers	4·95	2·02	2·93	1 : 1·45
Mistris	4·19	1·31	2·88	1 : 2·20
Munshis	5·15	1·56	3·59	1 : 2·30
Overall	4·76	1·63	3·13	1 : 1·92

*Family has been taken to include the respondent, his wife and children, and first degree relatives dependent on him irrespective of their place of residence.
**J. F. Bulsara, *Problems of Rapid Urbanization in India*, p.14.
The following table is given on the size of the family:

City	Size of family of Residents	Immigrants
Baroda	5·0	4·0
Gorakhpur	5·0	4·4
Hubli	5·8	4·8

APPENDIX-B

There were more earners in workers' families than the other two groups. The dependency load per earner was the lowest for workers, and the highest for the munshi group. Though families of munshis had more earners than mistris, the dependency load on earners in the former group remained higher due to the larger size of families. Again, 60 per cent of the workers' families had more than one earner, but 72 per cent of the mistris' families had one earner only. The dependency load was the highest in the munshi group where the earner-dependent ratio was 1:4 in 33 per cent of the cases.

Earnings

The respondents were asked to state their 'take-home' pay (as there were no other deductions, it was gross earnings less *peshgi*) during the month preceding that in which interviews took place. The responses are presented in Tables 9 and 10.*

TABLE 9

Table showing family income, income per earner and per capita income of respondents by job status

Category	Average monthly income (Rs.)		
	Per family	Per earner	Per capita
Workers	80·80	40·00	16·34
Mistris	203·05	155·00	48·50
Munshis	118·56	76·00	22·63
Overall	146·70	90·00	30·80

TABLE 10

Table showing levels of income of respondents by job status

Income group	Overall	Number of families		
		Workers	Mistris	Munshis
1. Less than Rs. 100 p.m.	25	28	5	18
2. Rs. 100-150 p.m.	34	39	8	20
3. Rs. 150-200 p.m.	20	18	41	24
4. Rs. 200 and more p.m.	21	15	46	38

*It was found that workers often did not tell or were incapable of telling what their family incomes were. The income data presented here deal mainly with their earnings from construction work and indicate at least their minimum incomes.

Table 9 brings out that the monthly family income of the worker group was the lowest in spite of the fact that families in this group had more earners than any other group. This was due to the relatively lower wage rates paid to them. In the munshi group, though an earner earned about twice as much as a worker, the family income and the per capita income were not correspondingly high due to the lesser number of earners per family and its larger size. The findings of Table 9 get further support from Table 10, wherein it was found that 46 per cent of mistris' and 58 per cent of munshis' families were in the income group of Rs. 200 and above; only 15 per cent of workers' families had less than Rs. 150 per month available to them.

The average per capita income of our respondents was Rs. 30·80 per month. The per capita income of a mistri was about three times that of a worker, and two times that of a munshi. The estimated average per capita income in Rajasthan was Rs. 23·25 per month. The contrast is indicative of the relatively higher earnings and the better economic conditions of the respondents, particularly the mistris. The data reveal considerable differences in the earnings of mistris and workers. Mistris' earnings in terms of family income as well as income per earner are four times higher than the workers' earnings. In Table 1 we have seen that even the minimum rate of wages fixed by the government for mistris was twice the rate for workers. Table 9 shows that whereas the mistris have been able to earn much more than the minimum fixed, the workers have difficulty even in maintaining the minimum standard. The reasons for this have been stated earlier. Short supply of skilled personnel, difficult working conditions in the construction industry, and craft grouping of mistris have pushed up their wages. On the contrary, the abundant labour supply maintained through the *jamadari* and the *peshgi* systems, and the unskilled nature of jobs, permit conditions wherein workers' rates of wages get pushed to levels lower than the minimum.

Migration

It has been reported in an earlier section that only 20·7 per cent of workers, 12·8 per cent of mistris, and 29·4 per cent of munshis belonged to Kota town or district. The rest of the group were immigrants. Of the immigrant workers, 61 per cent belonged to Rajasthan, and 39 per cent came from other States. The Rajasthani labour came mainly from the Jaipur, Jodhpur, and Ajmer districts. The non-Rajasthani labour was drawn from the Telangana districts of Andhra Pradesh, and the Saurashtra region of Gujarat. Seventy-six per cent immigrant mistris originated from States other than Rajasthan. They came from the Punjab, Delhi, western U.P., the Saurashtra region of Gujarat, the Khandesh district of Maharashtra, and Andhra Pradesh.

The respondents were asked to state the reasons for their migration to Kota. Eighty-six per cent of them were recruited for work at Kota, eight per cent came on transfer, two per cent originally came for trading purposes but drifted to construction jobs, and the remaining four per cent came for a variety of other reasons. An analysis of responses by job status did not show any significant variation from an overall analysis excepting that mistris reported 15 per cent of responses under the 'miscellaneous' category.

Almost all mistris stated that they elected to serve in this industry because their skill was appropriate and wages were better. More than three-fourths of the munshis reported that they worked in the construction industry because of lack of opportunities elsewhere. Another 11 per cent stated that they had worked with their current employers for long periods, and would not like to work for anyone else. The workers gave multiple answers for joining the construction industry as presented below:

To get better wages	14 per cent
Present work fits in with the pattern of work in agriculture	31 per cent
Got committed through *peshgi* and cannot get out of it	17 per cent
This is the only work I can do and get	24 per cent
Miscellaneous	14 per cent

Table 11 shows the manner in which the respondents were recruited to do the work they were currently engaged in.

The sources of vacancy information for workers stood in sharp contrast to that of mistris. Whereas 76 per cent of workers used informal and traditional sources to get jobs, almost the

TABLE 11

Table showing in percentage the distribution of respondents according to the sources of vacancy information (for immigrants only)

Source	Overall	By job status		
		Workers	Mistris	Munshis
1. Relatives, Friends	63·8	76·4	14·7	27·0
2. Employers' Agents (not Jamadars)	12·9	11·4	8·8	25·0
3. Direct Enquiry	11·2	9·2	20·6	14·6
4. Employment Exchanges, Advertisements, etc.	7·3	0·7	44·1	18·7
5. No Answer	4·8	2·2	11·7	14·6

same percentage of mistris used formal and structured sources of vacancy information. Munshis utilized all available sources with equal facility.

The process of migration also varied according to the job status of respondents. Sixty-two per cent of married workers moved to Kota along with their families; this implied that those who came alone in the beginning sent for their families soon thereafter. Seventy-four per cent of married mistris had their families living with them. But only 23 per cent brought their families along with them at the time of their first reporting for duty at Kota. More than half of the married immigrant munshis did not have their families living with them.

At the time of migration, only 22 per cent of respondents planned to settle down at Kota. Another 20 per cent had plans to go back on completion of the assignment, 39 per cent had no plans but knew they did not want to stay on at Kota, and the remaining 19 per cent either did not reply or gave no meaningful answer.

Work Experience

The study revealed that 36·4 per cent of respondents had no previous employment experience. This included 37 per cent of workers, 40 per cent of mistris, and 50 per cent of munshis. Of the remaining 63·6 per cent, 46 per cent had worked in the construction industry prior to their current jobs. The previous employments of the workers were in construction only. The munshis reported that they had held jobs previously but indicated specific industries. A total of 658 previous jobs were held by 230 employees giving an average of three jobs per person. Of the total number of previous jobs held by workers, as many as 521 were in the construction industry at Kota. Since the length of residence of 84 per cent of the workers at Kota did not exceed three years, these jobs were obviously done within this period which indicates the migratory nature of the respondents.

It was also found that the majority of the respondents took up their jobs when they were below 20 years of age. One-third of the workers could not tell their age at the time of starting their first job. Of the remaining, seven per cent were working before they were 20 years old. Only 30·8 per cent of mistris, and 26·4 per cent of munshis held jobs before completing 20 years of age. This is shown in Table 12.

TABLE 12

Table showing in percentage the distribution of respondents by age at the time of joining the first job

Age group	Overall	By job status		
		Workers	Mistris	Munshis
1. Less than 20 years	43·3	48·1	30·8	26·4
2. 20-30 years	18·2	16·0	28·3	23·5
3. 30-40 years	1·3	1·4	2·5	—
4. 40 years and above	1·1	1·7	—	—
5. Not available	35·8	32·8	38·4	50·0

The workers reported no unemployment spells. When jobs could not be found in the construction industry, they went back to their villages and worked in agriculture and allied industries. During lean agricultural years, they moved to other places and kept themselves engaged with whatever came their way. Some of them reported that they had worked even when migrating. They covered the distance on foot or on animal carts, and did odd jobs *en route*.

The mistris also reported no unemployment during the four years preceding the study. However, 52 per cent of mistris said that they had experienced frictional unemployment. The study made it obvious that workers found it prudent to maintain their village and land ties. In fact, 53 per cent of workers sent 30 to 45 per cent of their earnings back home. Only 12 per cent of respondents had any experience of work in industries other than agriculture and construction.

The trend in occupational mobility over two generations of respondents' families were also studied and are presented in Table 13.

TABLE 13

Table showing in percentage the occupational mobility of respondents' two preceding generations

Occupation	Workers G. Fathers	Workers Fathers	Mistris G. Fathers	Mistris Fathers	Munshis G. Fathers	Munshis Fathers
1. Agricultural & Allied	72	58	38	23	46	25
2. Non-Agricultural Labour	5	9	0	0	0	2
3. Artisan/Craftsman	9	9	5	5	7	9
4. Professions and Civil Service	2	10	6	26	13	28
5. Trade and Commerce	5	7	23	18	21	22
6. Technical/Mechanical	1	2	5	10	0	2
7. Others	3	5	5	0	7	12
8. Not Available	3	0	18	18	0	0

Table 13 reveals that the majority of workers came from agricultural stock, and mistris and munshis from white-collar families. The fathers of 58 per cent of workers were agriculturists but the fathers of 44 per cent of mistris, and of 50 per cent of munshis held white-collar jobs. The table also shows a tendency for a craftsman's son to follow the family craft. The families of non-agricultural labourers produced no mistris, and only an occasional munshi. Comparing the occupations of the grandfathers and fathers of the respondents, we observe a shift from agriculture to white-collar jobs, and an additional movement towards technical work in the case of mistris.

PERCEPTION OF THE JOB MARKET

Finally we come to the respondents' perception of the job market. An attempt will be made to examine their image of the mechanics of job market operations, and the way they rate themselves in it. Further, we will try to find out whether the exposure to employment in the construction industry at Kota brought any significant changes in their perception of the job market.

On Securing Jobs

The respondents were asked to state the sources of vacancy information in respect of their current jobs. They were further asked the question, 'How will you try to get a job if your current employment terminates?' Responses to both the questions are presented in Table 14.

TABLE 14

Table showing in percentage the distribution of respondents according to the sources of vacancy information in respect of current and future jobs

Source	Workers Current job	Workers Next job	Mistris Current job	Mistris Next job	Munshis Current job	Munshis Next job
1. Relatives and Friends	78·2	12·0	16·3	5·5	70·2	10·8
2. Employers' agents	11·7	1·4	9·7	—	12·1	1·0
3. Direct enquiry with Employers	9·3	68·2	22·5	35·2	10·6	58·3
4. Employment Exchanges & Advertisements	0·8	14·7	48·3	59·3	6·7	26·2
5. Miscellaneous	—	4·7	3·0	—	0·4	3·7
6. No Answer	—	—	—	—	—	—

Table 14 shows that 78·2 per cent of workers and 70·2 per cent of munshis secured their current jobs through relatives and friends. However, only 12 per cent of workers and 10·8 per cent of munshis expected to use this source to secure employment in future. Direct enquiries with employers were expected to be resorted to by 68·2 per cent of workers and 58·3 per cent of munshis. Thus, we find a major shift in the sources of vacancy information in the case of workers and munshis. Their stay at Kota seems to have given them wider contacts and information about the possibilities of employment. Informal and traditional sources of vacancy information prove useful only to 16·3 per cent of mistris, and they would not regard such methods as significant for the future. Almost all mistris expected to use either direct enquiry with employers or employment exchanges or vacancy advertisements for employment in the future. An increasing number of workers and munshis also pinned their hopes in employment exchanges for future jobs.

The respondents were also asked: 'What will matter most in getting a job in future?' Seventy-two per cent replied 'education, training, and past experience'. This response group included 67 per cent of workers, 76 per cent of mistris, and 72 per cent of munshis. 'Contacts with those who matter', and 'ability to influence prospective employers' were considered important by 17 per cent of workers, 21 per cent of mistris, and 16 per cent of munshis. It is obvious from the data presented above that as a result of their current employment, the respondents had greater information of where jobs could be found. They thought they were better equipped for finding jobs on their own, and were more aware that skill was more important than 'pull' in getting a job.

Another set of questions put to respondents were: 'How much time did it take you to get the current job?', and 'How much time will it take to find another job, if you happen to get dismissed?' Their responses are presented in Table 15.

Table 15 lends itself to two major comments. First, an overwhelming majority of the respondents were sure that they would find alternative jobs if they lost the current ones. The uncertainty increased only with decrease in skill. Second, the respondents perceived a more favourable employment market obtaining at the time of the study as compared to the period when they took

TABLE 15

Table showing percentage distribution of respondents according to time taken to get the current job and expected time required to find a new job

Period	Workers Current job	Workers Next job	Mistris Current job	Mistris Next job	Munshis Current job	Munshis Next job
1. Less than one month	8·6	31·5	24·5	28·9	6·6	27·3
2. Less than six months	49·4	39·1	55·6	44·7	25·6	40·3
3. More than six months	34·0	3·8	17·4	13·2	66·8	8·9
4. Did not remember	8·0	—	2·5	—	1·0	—
5. Not sure	—	25·6	—	13·2	—	23·5

up their current jobs. Only 8·6 per cent of workers got their current jobs within one month, against a future possibility of this period perceived by 31·5 per cent. In fact, all those who thought they could find alternative jobs were also sure that they would find them within six months. The present work experience gave confidence to the workers that jobs were not difficult to find.

Job Preference

Respondents were asked to indicate their preferences in terms of industries they liked to work in. Sixty-three per cent each of workers and mistris, and 57 per cent of munshis had no preferences. Only two per cent of workers, three per cent of mistris, and no munshi expressed a desire to work in some other industry; the remaining wanted to work in construction only. Seventy-nine per cent of the total sample was willing to work in any part of the country. It is interesting to note that almost all local respondents, irrespective of their job status, wanted to work at Kota only. They were further asked about the highest salary level that they desired to achieve, and whether they expected to achieve it and, if so, how much time would it take. The aspirations were rather modest, perhaps realistic. Only 24·6 per cent of workers aspired to earn more than Rs. 200 a month.

Another 44·5 per cent considered Rs. 150-200 a month as desirable, and the rest aspired to even lower wages. Eighty-five per cent supervisors aspired to earn more than Rs. 200 a month. In the case of munshis, the aspiration level was over Rs. 200 a month for 42·3 per cent, between Rs. 150 and 200 a month for 46·2 per cent, and below Rs. 150 a month for 11·5 per cent. Ninety per cent of respondents, evenly distributed by job status, felt that they could achieve the aspired salary levels, but differed regarding the time that it would take. Fifty-seven per cent of workers, 54 per cent of munshis, and only 32 per cent of mistris hoped that they could achieve what they expected in less than four years. However, 29 per cent of the total respondents were uncertain about the time required. The respondents also differed as to what was required for achieving the aspired level. Demonstrated merit found favour with 60 per cent of workers, 19 per cent of mistris, and 65 per cent of munshis. Seniority was considered important by 72 per cent of mistris, and an insignificant number in the other two groups. The 'ability to be on the right side of the boss' was uniformly low in rating—at 7 per cent—by all the groups. Thus, the majority of the respondents had no set preferences for industries they wanted to work in. Immigrants were prepared to work anywhere.

The respondents aspired to work in positions carrying remuneration that was only a little higher than what they earned currently. Most of them expected to achieve the desired level of earnings within four years. Whereas most of the workers and the munshis hoped to achieve the desired goal by demonstrated merit, mistris thought it important to establish seniority.

Education and Training

The study revealed that the current job experience of respondents generated sufficient awareness of the value of higher education and further training. Only 13·4 per cent of workers were not sure that they wanted further education. If it were possible, 56·5 per cent of them would like to qualify for high school, 17·9 per cent would go in for graduate studies, and 2·9 per cent for technical courses. Those who wanted education up to high school were motivated by the desire to understand their environment, wage payments, etc. Higher studies were sought for civil service jobs. All but 0·3 per cent of workers knew specifically why they wanted further education and believed it would improve their social and economic conditions. It was also found that 64·2 per cent of mistris desired to go in for a professional degree/diploma course. Regarding munshis, 57·4 per cent wanted to qualify for the B.A. degree and secure better white-collar jobs.

In order further to explore the importance that the respondents attached to education, they were asked the question: 'How much education would you like to give to your son?' Two-thirds of mistris and half of munshis said that they would want their sons to go in for a degree/diploma course in technical or engineering subjects. However, 43·4 per cent thought their sons should go through high school, and another 26·5 per cent were not sure what their sons should train for.

As regards training, 70 per cent of workers, and 64·7 per cent of munshis felt that the possibilities of future promotions were independent of any training. However, all those who perceived training as necessary for their promotions desired technical training only, and were not bothered about the place or the form of training so long as their expenses were met. It appears that workers perceived education as basic to their progress, but were relatively less emphatic on training. Where they did attach importance to training they displayed a bias towards technical training.

Choice of Occupation

The respondents were asked whether they would opt to continue to work in the construction industry if it were possible somehow to free them of all financial worries. They were further asked to state reasons for their answer, and if they desired not to work in the construction industry, what kind of work would they do. Of the total respondents, 58·2 per cent said that they would not work in the construction industry. This included 54·2 per cent of workers, 64·1 per cent of mistris, and 60·3 per cent of munshis. In order of preferred occupation of those who wanted to shift, 59·3 per cent of workers would like to do farming, 34·6 per cent independent work such as craft, retail trade, etc., and another 6·1 per cent factory jobs. Ninety-three per cent of mistris would like not to work for anyone but to set up independent establishments. Among munshis, 66·5 per cent wanted to do retail trade or craftsmanship, 15·2 per cent farming, and 7·2 per cent factory jobs.

Conclusions

1. The construction industry as defined in the first section is one of the major operations at Kota. It is characterized by a very low level of technology, seasonal and temporary work, gang labour, and wage rates lower than those for production workers in the area. Almost the entire workforce is employed on a contract basis and paid, mostly, piece-rate wages. Protective measures pertaining to health, safety, welfare, working hours, and working conditions are difficult to enforce and implement.

2. Recruitment of workers is done through intermediaries, called jamadars. The contractors keep their hold on the jamadars as well as the workers through the *peshgi* system. The jamadari and the *peshgi* systems may appear to be socially undesirable, yet they meet the peculiar needs of the industry and its workers. Because of these systems, the contractors can recruit the required strength of labour and maintain a surplus labour pool, and workers may, hopefully, find employment when their presence is not required in agriculture. The construction industry largely supplements employment in agriculture. Due to the scarcity of skilled personnel, and relatively more comfortable working conditions in the manufacturing industries, the construction employers find it difficult to recruit high-skilled personnel. This is a disadvantage which they try to overcome by offering a comparatively much higher wage rate and by encouraging personal loyalties of the mistris to the 'high-ups' in the companies. The recruitment of munshis is not considered a problem by any company. A good number of persons are locally available, and can be had by calling at the employment exchange.

3. In some of its operations, the construction industry resembles agriculture. It calls for strong muscles, requires

outdoor work, permits reward by results, and encourages the concept of family employment and gang labour. An agricultural worker can transfer himself from land to construction and become productive without loss of time.

4. The social organization of the construction industry is based on village and caste factors. The occupational hierarchy corresponds with the traditional caste hierarchy. Superior and clean jobs are mostly held by mistris and munshis who belong to higher castes, while the great majority of workers are Harijans. The reasons for the existence of caste hierarchy in this industry appear to be more economic than social. The majority of workers are immigrants coming from agriculturally non-productive districts where the landless labour also happened to belong to the lower castes. It is natural for the lowest economic and social status groups to be the first amongst those who are pushed out from the villages.

5. In any portrayal of the three occupational groups in this industry, their social attributes stand out with considerable distinctness. The worker is mostly a young agriculturist, illiterate, of rural background, unskilled, immigrant, Harijan, having a medium size family with more earners but less family income. He started earning when less than 20 years old, and had changed about three jobs prior to the current one. His village provides him with both economic and societal security, and he returns to it as often as he can, or when city dwelling becomes non-remunerative. Since more hands mean more work and higher earnings, he migrates with his family.

The mistri more often is in his thirties, educated, skilled, and belongs to the white-collar, urban, high caste family. He has a relatively smaller family, one earner, but higher income. He too is an immigrant, and entered the job when about 25 years old.

The munshi is an educated unskilled local urbanite, who belongs to a traditionally white-collar family. His family is large, with less number of earners and low income. He is in his thirties, and started earning in his early twenties.

6. On an average, a respondent earned Rs. 90 per month. The monthly earnings of a mistri were Rs. 155, of a worker Rs. 40, and of a munshi Rs. 76. The workers compensated their low earnings by putting more hands of the family to work. The family income of a worker worked out to Rs. 80·80 per month against Rs. 118·56 of a munshi. The difference in the total earnings of the workers and the munshis, in spite of the fact that the worker puts in more hands, is due to the difference in wage rates of the two categories. These figures do not include earnings from the land.

7. As workers combined construction jobs with agricultural work, they neither reported nor perceived any unemployment. Mistris likewise did not report any unemployment during the four years preceding the enquiry, and suffered only frictional unemployment during the earlier periods. This situation may be due to the fact that industry at Kota is expanding rapidly, resulting in greater job opportunities.

8. Very few workers had experience of work in the organized sectors of industry. They oscillated between agriculture and construction. The data also bring out a significant movement of respondents' families from agriculture to white-collar jobs over two generations. The families of mistris had moved towards technical professions more rapidly than the other groups. However, it was also found that a craftsman's son tended to follow his father's occupation.

9. The experience of work in the construction industry developed in workers only limited potentialities of becoming members of a permanent industrial workforce. A significant change has occurred in their sources of vacancy information, perception of job market, and attitude towards education and training. Whereas most of the workers secured their present jobs through friends and relatives, they are now more confident of finding future jobs on their own. They perceive that jobs are available. They know where they lie, and with whom and how to make contact for the purpose. They feel that education and work experience,

and training to a lesser extent, matter most in getting a better job. But the concept of 'better job' involves slightly higher earnings as compared to what they earn now. Most of the workers expect to reach the desired level and nature of work within four years. In short, workers are better informed of job market conditions, are confident that they will not remain unemployed, and expect to achieve the desired positions. Knowledge, confidence, and hope are the three principal benefits that their present jobs have given them.

10. Our study shows that though the workers took up jobs in the construction industry, they did not commit themselves to it. They worked out a logical arrangement to secure continuity in their earnings. The land and the village serve as their backbone, and give permanent security. They opted for this arrangement in spite of their perception of a seller's employment market.

But then the construction industry does not provide conditions in which workers experience a social and work environment that is basically different from agriculture. The jamadari and *peshgi* systems, the unregulated working conditions, the intermittent employment, etc., are also aspects of their traditional work. Neither does the industry provide any alternat've mechanism to meet those needs of workers that are currently met by the traditional system. Therefore, we draw attention to the conditions necessary to set in motion the processes that would help people to begin to perceive themselves as industrial workers. Regulation of employment and working conditions through legislative action, licensing of jamadars and other recruiting agents, elimination of the *peshgi* system, and securing for workers continuity of employment similar to that assured for those employed in manufacturing industries, are the initial steps in that direction. Stabilization of the construction workforce at new townships may be attempted by providing houses, schools, and medical care to workers and their families as provided in the plantations.

Before concluding, we would also like to draw attention to the need for a planned rural-urban balance. The study shows that in general only the young and literate are moving out of villages, and away from agriculture. A country whose base of economy is agriculture cannot afford the weaning away of the cream of its agricultural workforce.

Appendix—C

A SELECT BIBLIOGRAPHY OF STUDIES ON INDUSTRIAL TOWNS AND SOCIAL CHANGE IN INDIA

Industrial Towns

1. BALAKRISHNA, R. *Report on the economic survey of Madras city* (1954-57). Delhi, Manager of Publications, 1961.
2. BOARD OF ECONOMIC ENQUIRY, PUNJAB. *Economic survey of industrial labour in the Punjab.* The author, 1950. viii, 173 p.
3. BOPEGAMAGE, A. *Delhi : a study in urban sociology.* Bombay, University of Bombay, 1957.
4. BOPEGAMAGE, A. and VEERARAGHAVAN, P. V. *Status images in changing India : a study based on two surveys.* Bombay, Manaktalas, 1967. x, 212 p.
5. CHAUHAN, D. S. *Trends of urbanization in Agra.* Bombay, Allied, 1966. 459 p.
6. DELHI ADMINISTRATION. INDUSTRIES (DIRECTORATE OF—). *Second industrial survey of Delhi—1964 : Okhla industrial estate.* Delhi, 1966. 63 p. (mimeographed.)
7. DHEKNEY, B. R. *Hubli city : a study in urban economic life.* Dharwar, Karnatak University, 1959. xx, 281 p.
8. GADGIL, D. R. *Sholapur city : socio-economic studies.* Poona, Gokhale Institute of Politics and Economics, 1965. xii, 337 p. (Gokhale Institute studies, no. 46.)
9. INDIA. FINANCE (MINISTRY OF—). ECONOMIC AFFAIRS (DEPARTMENT OF—). *Survey of Faridabad township, March-April,* 1954. The author, 1954. iv, 155 p. (National Sample Survey, no. 6.)
10. IYENGAR, S. KESAVA. *Socio-economic survey of Hyderabad-Secunderabad city area.* Hyderabad, Indian Institute of Economics, 1957.
11. LAKDAWALA, D. T. and others. *Work, wages and well-being in an Indian metropolis : economic survey of Bombay city.* Bombay, University of Bombay, 1963. vi, 863 p. (University of Bombay, series in economics, no. 11.)

12. LAKDAWALA, D. T. and SANDESARA, J. C. *Small-industry in a big city—a survey in Bombay.* Bombay, University of Bombay, 1960. xvi, 387 p. (University of Bombay, series in economics, no. 10.)
13. LAMBERT, RICHARD D. *Workers, factories and social change in India.* Bombay, Asia, 1963. xiii, 247 p.
14. MADHYA PRADESH. ECONOMICS AND STATISTICS (DIRECTORATE OF—). *Socio-economic survey of Bhilai region.* Pt. 1, first round, 1955-56. Bombay, Popular, 1959. xvi, 356 p.
15. MAJUMDAR, D. N. *Social contours of an industrial city—social survey of Kanpur*, 1954-56. Bombay, Asia, 1960. xxiv, 242 p.
16. MALHOTRA, P. C. *Socio-economic survey of Bhopal city and Bhairagarh.* Bombay, Asia, 1964. v, 404 p.
17. MALKANI, H. C. *Socio-economic survey of Baroda city.* Baroda, M. S. University of Baroda, 1958. xi, 179 p.
18. MISRA, B. R. *Socio-economic survey of Jamshedpur city.* Patna, Patna University, 1959. v, 134 p.
19. MOHSIN, MOHAMMAD. *Chittaranjan : a study in urban sociology.* Bombay, Popular, 1964. vi, 198 p.
20. MORRIS, MORRIS DAVID. *Emergence of an industrial labour force in India : a study of the Bombay cotton textile mills*, 1854-1947. Berkeley, University of California Press, 1965. xiii, 263 p.
21. MUKERJEE, RADHAKAMAL and SINGH, BALJIT. *District town in transition : social and economic survey of Gorakhpur.* Bombay, Asia, 1965. xii, 187 p.
22. MUKERJEE, RADHAKAMAL and SINGH, BALJIT. *Social profiles of a metropolis : social and economic structure of Lucknow, capital of Uttar Pradesh*, 1954-56. Bombay, Asia, 1961. xii, 210 p.
23. PATEL, KUNJ. *Rural labour in industrial Bombay.* Bombay, Popular, 1963. ix, 191 p.
24. PATIL, R. K. and TALATI, K. M. *Surat : a socio-economic survey, a study in trends in urbanization.* Surat, Chunilal Gandhi Institute of Learning and Research, 1957. 59, 19, 31 p. (unpublished.)
25. PUNJAB. ECONOMIC AND STATISTICAL ORGANIZATION.

Chandigarh : *socio-economic survey conducted in May*, 1957. The author, 1957. 54 p. (mimeographed.)

26. RAJAGOPALAN, C. *Greater Bombay* : *a study in suburban ecology*. Bombay, Popular, 1962. xxii, 211 p.

27. RAO, V. K. R. V. and DESAI, P. B. *Greater Delhi* : *a study in urbanization*—1940-1957. Bombay, Asia, 1965. xxxiii, 479 p.

28. SEN, S. N. *City of Calcutta* : *a socio-economic survey*, 1954-55 *to* 1957-58. Calcutta, Bookland Private Limited, 1960. ii, 271 p.

29. SOVANI, N. V. and others. *Poona* : *a resurvey*; *the changing pattern of employment and earning*. Poona, Gokhale Institute of Politics and Economics, 1956. xx, 555 p., (Gokhale Institute of Politics and Economics publications, 34.)

30. SOVANI, N. V. *Social survey of Kolhapur city*. Poona, Gokhale Institute of Politics and Economics. 3V.
    V. 1. 1948. x, 79 p.
    V. 2. 1951. x, 346 p.
    V. 3. 1952. xiv, 330 p.

31. UNESCO RESEARCH CENTRE ON THE SOCIAL IMPLICATIONS OF INDUSTRIALISATION IN SOUTHERN ASIA, CALCUTTA. *Social implications of industrialization and urbanization, five studies in Asia*. Calcutta, the Centre, 1956. xi, 268 p.

32. UNESCO RESEARCH CENTRE ON SOCIAL AND ECONOMIC DEVELOPMENT IN SOUTHERN ASIA, DELHI. *Social and cultural factors affecting productivity of industrial workers in India*. Delhi, the Centre, 1961. ii, 127, 51 p.

SOCIAL CHANGE

33. AIYAPPAN, A. *Social revolution in a Kerala village* : *a study in culture change*. Bombay, Asia, 1965. x, 183 p.

34. BAILEY, F. G. *Caste and the economic frontier* : *a village in highland Orissa*. Bombay, Oxford University Press, 1958. xvi, 292 p.

35. DESAI, A. R. *Rural India in transition*. Bombay, Popular, 1961. x, 183 p.

36. DESAI, I. P. *Some aspects of family in Mahuva* : *a sociolo-*

gical study of jointness in a small town. Bombay, Asia, 1964. xii, 239 p.

37. DUBE, S. C. *India's changing villages : human factors in community development.* London, Routledge & Kegan Paul, 1958. xii, 230 p.

38. EPSTEIN, T. SCARLETT. *Economic development and social change in South India.* Bombay, Oxford University Press, 1962. xvi, 353 p.

39. GHURYE, G. S. *After a century and a quarter : Lonikand then and now.* Bombay, Popular, 1960. xl, 126 p.

40. GUPTA, S. C. *Economic survey of Shamaspur village (District Saharanpur, Uttar Pradesh), a case study in the structure and functioning of a village economy.* Bombay, Asia, 1959. viii, 148 p.

41. INDIAN INSTITUTE OF PUBLIC ADMINISTRATION, NEW DELHI. *Perspectives : studies in social and political forecasting.* New Delhi, the Institute, 1965. 98 p. (Supplement to the Indian Journal of Public Administration, V. xi, no. 1, January-March, 1965.)

42. INDIAN SOCIETY OF AGRICULTURAL ECONOMICS, BOMBAY. *Bhadkad, social and economic survey of a village : a comparative study, 1915-1955.* Bombay, the Society, 1957. vii, 71 p.

43. ISHWARAN, K. *Tradition and economy in village India.* Bombay, Allied, 1966. xiv, 169 p.

44. MARRIOTT, MCKIM. *Village India : studies in the little community.* Chicago, University of Chicago, 1955. xix, 269 p.

45. MAYER, ALBERT and associates. *Pilot project, India : the story of rural development at Etawah, Uttar Pradesh.* Berkeley, University of California Press, 1958. xxiv, 367 p.

46. NAG, D. S. *Tribal economy : an economic study of the Baiga.* Delhi, Bhartiya Adimjati Sevak Sangh, 1958. xvii, 418 p.

47. NATIONAL COUNCIL OF APPLIED ECONOMIC RESEARCH, NEW DELHI. *Socio-economic conditions of primitive tribes of Madhya Pradesh.* New Delhi, the Council, 1963. xviii, 206 p.

48. PANDIT, D. P. *Earning one's livelihood in Mahuva.* Bombay, Asia, 1965. xii, 96 p.
49. RAO, M. S. A. *Social change in Malabar.* Bombay, Popular, 1957. vi, 228 p.
50. SACHCHIDANANDA. *Culture change in tribal Bihar : Munda and Oraon.* Calcutta, Bookland Private Limited, 1964. 158 p.
51. SIVERTSEN, DAGFINN. *When caste barriers fall : a study of social and economic change in a South Indian village.* New York, Humanities Press, 1963. 141 p.
52. SRINIVAS, M. N. *Social change in modern India.* Bombay, Allied, 1966. xv, 194 p.
53. VIDYARATHI, L. P. *Cultural contours of tribal Bihar.* Calcutta, Punthi Pustak, 1964. xx, 308 p.
54. WEST BENGAL. DEVELOPMENT DEPARTMENT. *India's villages.* Calcutta, West Bengal Government Press, 1955. 198 p.

RAJASTHAN

55. CHABRA P. C. and MISHRA, R. K., *eds. Rajasthan : a decade of reconstruction,* 1954-64. Jaipur, Pratibha Prakashan, 1965. xxiv, 152 p.
56. CHAUHAN, BRIJ RAJ. *Rajasthan village.* New Delhi, Vir Publishing House, 1967. viii, 338 p.
57. DANDIA, MILAP CHAND, *ed. Rajasthan year book and who is who.* Jaipur, Sammriddhi Publications, 1963.
58. INDIA. REGISTRAR GENERAL (OFFICE OF THE—). *Census of India,* 1951. Vol. 1, pt. II-A : demographic tables. Delhi, Manager of Publications, 1955.
59. INDIA. REGISTRAR GENERAL (OFFICE OF THE—). *Census of India,* 1961. Paper no. 1, 1962 : final population tables. Delhi, Manager of Publications, 1962. xvi, 454 p.
60. INDIA. REGISTRAR GENERAL (OFFICE OF THE—). *Census of India,* 1961. Vol. 1, pt. II-A(1) : general population tables. Delhi, Manager of Publications, 1964. vi, 691 p.
61. IMPERIAL GAZETTEER OF INDIA. *Provincial series, Rajputana.* Calcutta, Government Press, 1908.
62. KATIYAR, T. S. *Social life in Rajasthan : a case study.* Allahabad, Kitab Mahal, 1964. vi, 127 p.
63. NATIONAL COUNCIL OF APPLIED ECONOMIC RESEARCH,

NEW DELHI. *Techno-economic survey of Rajasthan.* New Delhi, the Council, 1963. xvi, 316 p.

64. RAJASTHAN. CENSUS OPERATIONS (SUPERINTENDENT OF—). *Census of India,* 1961. Vol. XIV, pt. II-A : general population tables. Delhi, Manager of Publications, 1964. viii, 230 p.

65. RAJASTHAN. CENSUS OPERATIONS (SUPERINTENDENT OF—). *Census of India,* 1961. Vol. XIV, pt. II-B : general economic tables. Delhi, Manager of Publications, 1965. 2 Pts.

66. RAJASTHAN. CENSUS OPERATIONS (SUPERINTENDENT OF—). *Census of India,* 1961. Vol. XIV, pt. VI-A (3) : Sanwara, a village survey monograph. Delhi, Manager of Publications, 1965. 46 p.

67. RAJASTHAN. CENSUS OPERATIONS (SUPERINTENDENT OF—). *Census of India,* 1961. Vol. XIV, pt. VII-A(i) : selected survey of crafts—Badla of Jodhpur, carpet of Jaipur, wooden toys of Udaipur and lapidary work of Jaipur. Delhi, Manager of Publications, 1966. iv, 105 p.

68. RAJASTHAN. ECONOMICS AND STATISTICS (DIRECTORATE OF—). *Basic statistics,* 1960 *and* 1963. Jaipur, the Author.

69. RAJASTHAN. ECONOMICS AND STATISTICS (DIRECTORATE OF—). Industrial structure of Rajasthan, 1961. Jaipur, the Author, 1964. ii, 126 p.

70. RAJASTHAN. ECONOMICS AND STATISTICS (DIRECTORATE OF—). *Rajasthan : a decade of planned economy.* Jaipur, the Author, 1962. 43 p.

71. RAJASTHAN. ECONOMICS AND STATISTICS (DIRECTORATE OF—). *Statistical abstract,* 1958 *and* 1962. Jaipur, the Author.

72. RAJASTHAN. LABOUR DEPARTMENT. *Progress of labour in Rajasthan.* Jaipur, Directorate of Public Relations, 1964. 24 p.

INDEX

Absenteeism 12, 17, 76
Age group 11, 12, 13, 14, 34-5, 44, 45, 46, 49, 50, 64, 82, 85-6, 90, 92, 131, 132, 163-4, 173, 181, 184
Agricultural labour 133, 155, 158, 174, 181, 182, 184
Ajmer 171
Alternative jobs 61, 67
Ancillary jobs 48
Andhra Pradesh 171
Approved List of Contractors 154
Assistant Director of Industries 151n
Attitudinal change 64, 70

Baroda 168n
Beldars 154, 156, 157, 163
Bombay 29
Brahmins 38, 167
Bulsara, J. F. 168n

Caste 5, 11, 12, 13, 14, 34, 38, 45, 47, 49, 53, 82, 87-8, 90, 104, 133, 138, 160, 161, 166-7, 181
Casual work 45
Census of India, 1951 22n
Census of India, 1961 21n, 22n, 45n
Central Public Works Department Rules 154
Chambal Hydro-Electric Project 21

Chambal Valley Project 151, 152, 153
Chambal river 21, 152
Chambal Workshop 23
Chi Square Test 77
Christians 166, 167
Civil services 4, 9, 15, 37, 41, 42, 112, 135, 174, 179
Clerks 10, 13, 14, 16, 17, 26, 27, 28, 30, 31, 35, 36, 38, 39, 60, 67, 68, 70, 81, 89, 110, 128, 129, 135, 154, 157, 163, 165
Collective bargaining 137
Community services 10
Construction industry 154-63
Construction worker 151-84
Contract of Agreement 158
Cultivators 41, 42, 49, 174, 181
Cultural inadequacy 46-7, 49, 131

Dandia, Milap Chand 21n
Delhi 29, 171
Dependency load 12, 14, 39, 49, 83, 88-9, 90, 106, 131, 169
Division of labour 4

Economic development 2, 45, 138
Education level 11, 13, 35-6, 40, 41, 45, 46, 49, 51, 55, 62, 63, 66, 68, 94, 130, 131, 133, 134, 164-5, 176, 181, 184
Efficiency, Industrial 2, 6, 8, 9, 76

Employee adjustment to work 5-12, 13, 16, 20, 34, 71, 76-109, 119, 128-31, 135, 137, 138, 139, 141
  Characteristics 6-7
  Concept 5-6
  Influencing factors 7-12
  Institutional factors 7-10, 12, 80-82, 90, 110, 128-9
    Job status 9-10, 13, 76, 81-2, 83, 89, 90, 91, 128
    Ownership 8-9, 13, 76, 78-80, 128, 129
    Size of the plant 9, 13, 80-81, 89, 128
    Technology 7-8, 12, 76, 90
  Job factors 10, 11, 12, 13, 110, 129-30
  Socio-personal factors 11-2, 13, 14, 82-9, 90, 110, 130-31
Employee gradation 8
Employee-oriented measure 76
Employees' Provident Fund Scheme 138
Employees' State Insurance Scheme 138
Employment 7, 11, 13, 14, 17, 25, 26, 27, 44, 48, 60, 61, 68, 69, 113, 115, 118, 131, 132, 133, 134, 135, 137, 144, 153, 160, 161, 175, 176, 180, 183
Employment Exchange, Kota 23*n*
Employment Exchanges 62, 66, 138, 151*n*, 162, 163, 172, 175, 176
Employment experience 41, 56, 98, 130, 143, 152, 172-5, 176, 182, 183

Employment security, see job security
Entrepreneurship 1
Excessive pay-roll 135

Factories Act, 1948 138
Factories, workers and social change in India, by R. D. Lambert 34*n*
Factory system 2-5, 6, 12, 20, 32, 49
Fair wage 158
Family 5, 10, 38, 39, 44, 45, 46, 53, 130, 132, 133, 138, 143, 155, 158, 167-8, 169, 172, 175, 181, 182, 183
Family income 39-41, 46, 54, 169, 170, 181, 182
Flow of work 3
Foreman 3
Fringe benefits 3, 10, 64, 70, 128, 132
From field to factory, by J. S. Slotkin 34*n*
Future jobs 62, 66, 67, 70

Gandhi Sagar 153
Gang labour 4, 155, 156, 157, 161, 180
Go-slow methods 3
Gorakhpur 168*n*
Grievances 3
Gujarat 171

Harijans 38, 47, 87, 131, 167, 181
Hindus 166, 167
Hiring labour 160
Hours of work 3, 10, 12, 26, 155, 158, 180

INDEX

Housing 5, 10, 12, 13, 26, 28, 70, 77, 110, 111, 112, 113, 114, 115, 116, 117, 118, 119, 129, 130, 132, 133, 135, 136, 138, 183
Hubli 168*n*
Human adjustment to work, see Employee adjustment to work

Immigration, see Migratory status
Imperial Gazetteer of India 21*n*
Incentives 6, 9, 12, 139
Income 11, 12, 13, 14, 46, 55, 61, 108
Indian Railway Service 27
Industrial conflicts 135
Industrial efficiency, see Efficiency, Industrial
Industrialization 1, 2, 24, 45, 71, 128, 131, 132, 133, 138, 139
Initiative 7, 8, 9
Innovation 9
Inspector of Factories 151*n*
Institutional factors 7-10, 12, 80-82, 90, 110, 128-9
Inter-personal relations 4

Jaipur 171
Jamadari commission 161
Jamadari system 160, 161, 170, 180, 183
Jamadars 154, 156, 157, 160-62, 163, 180, 183
Job Attitude Scale (JAS) 16, 77-8, 89, 150
Job changes 43-4, 58, 136, 179, 181
Job experience 44, 57, 60, 61, 82, 88, 90, 152, 178, 182, 183

Job factors 10-11, 12, 13, 110, 129-30
Job market 12, 20, 44, 49, 60, 75, 113, 134-6, 137, 145, 183
  Employee perception 60, 61-3, 70, 175-80, 182-83
  Entry 65-7
Job mobility 41, 44, 135, 152, 174
Job satisfaction 6, 130
Job security 3, 10, 13, 28, 35, 64, 70, 77, 110, 112, 113, 114, 115, 116, 117, 118, 119, 129, 130, 132, 133, 136, 138, 159
Job selection 63-4, 111, 118, 132, 136, 177-8, 179-80
Job status 7, 9-10, 13, 16, 17, 34, 35, 38, 39, 40, 50, 51, 53, 54, 60, 61, 67, 76, 81-2, 83, 89, 90, 91, 92, 93, 96, 98, 100, 102, 104, 106, 108, 119, 128, 130, 163, 164, 165, 166, 167, 168, 169, 171, 172, 177
Jobbers 65
Job *en route* 174
Jodhpur 171
Joint consultation 28

Khandesh 171
Kota Barrage 153
Kota town
  as case study 14-20
  Chemical industries 24, 25-6
  Demographic changes 22-4
  Factories 21-33
  Geography 21
  Social conditions 21-4
Kshatriyas 38, 167

Labour discipline 3, 12, 129, 133, 137

Labour legislation 118, 155, 156
Labour-management relations 2, 12, 156
Labour market 3, 44, 45, 48
Labour productivity 12, 48, 128
Labour turnover 17, 35, 76, 112
Labour unions, see Unionism
Lambert, R. D. 34*n*
Literacy level, see Education level
Lockouts 3

Management's role in industry 26, 137-9
Maharashtra 171
Managers 2, 3, 17, 25, 26, 27, 29
Mean Work Adjustment Score 77, 78, 80, 81, 83, 84, 85, 88
Migratory status 11, 12, 13, 14 34, 37-8, 40, 41, 45, 46, 47, 49, 55, 82, 87, 90, 100, 102, 130, 131, 133, 135, 166, 170-72, 181
Minimum Wages Act, 1948 158, 159
Minimum Wages Inspector 151*n*
Mistris 65, 154, 155, 156, 157, 162, 163, 164, 165, 166, 167, 168, 169, 170, 171, 172, 173, 174, 175, 176, 177, 178, 179, 180, 181, 182
Motivation 5, 139
Moghuls 21
Munshis 154, 155, 156, 157, 162-3, 164, 165, 166, 167, 168, 169, 170, 171, 172, 173, 174, 175, 176, 177, 178, 179, 180, 181, 182

Muslims 166

New worker 14, 118, 132-4, 161
Newspaper advertisements 62, 65, 69, 162, 164, 172, 175, 176

Occupational change 3, 4, 41-2, 45, 56, 174
Occupational seniority 28, 35
Operatives 2, 3, 4, 8, 13, 24, 42, 48, 90, 153
Opportunities for advancement, see Promotion
Organization-oriented measure 76
Organizational goals 9
Overall Mean Score 78, 83, 87
Overhead benefits 155
Ownership 7, 8-9, 12, 13, 15, 25, 76, 78-80, 89, 128, 192

Pay compensation 156
Pearson's Product Moment 77
Personal goals 9
Peshgi system 160, 161, 162, 169, 170, 171, 180, 183
Piece-rate system of payment 155, 158, 159, 180
Political parties 137
Princely states 21, 30, 37, 112
Private enterprise 7, 8, 9, 13, 15, 25, 35, 36, 42, 48, 49, 69, 80, 82, 86, 111, 112, 113, 114, 115, 118, 119, 129, 132, 136
Problem solving attitude 7
Problems of Rapid Urbanization in India, by J. F. Bulsara 168*n*
Profit 8, 154

INDEX

Promotions 8, 9, 10, 12, 13, 26, 27, 28, 35, 69, 70, 110, 112, 113, 114, 115, 116, 117, 118, 119, 129, 130, 131, 132, 133, 136, 179
Protective legislation 156, 180
Public enterprise 8, 9, 13, 15, 25, 35, 36, 42, 48, 49, 66, 80, 82, 111, 112, 113, 114, 115, 117, 118, 119, 129, 132, 136
Public utilities 30-31
Punjab 29, 171

Railway Board 27
Rajasthan 21, 29, 30, 34, 35, 36, 37, 38, 39, 40, 45, 46, 87, 131, 133, 164, 166, 168, 170, 171
Rajasthan. Economics & Statistics—Directorate of $22n$, $23n$
Rajasthan Government 17, 153, 158, 159
Rajasthan. Irrigation—Department of $151n$
Rajasthan. Public Works Department 30, $151n$, 165
Rajasthan. State Electricity Board 30
Rajasthan Year Book and Who is Who $21n$, $22n$
Recruitment 3, 9, 12, 26, 28, 29, 34, 35, 36, 38, 47-9, 70, 91, 115, 117, 119, 130, 134, 135, 157, 160, 162, 163, 171
Resignations 44

Saurashtra 171
Seasonal work 156, 180
Selection procedure 67
Shift work 158
Sikhs 166

Skilled workforce 3, 36-7, 42, 45, 48, 52, 82, 85, 89, 90, 96, 130, 131, 132, 133, 134, 135, 137, 153, 154, 155, 156, 162, 165, 170, 176, 180, 181
Slotkin, J. S. $34n$
Social justice 9
Social selectivity 45-6, 60, 131
Social structure 5, 6, 133
Socio-personal factors 11-2, 13, 14, 82-9, 90, 110, 130-31, 181
Spearman-Brown Formula 77
Statistical Abstract, Rajasthan $23n$
Strikes 3
Suggestion schemes 12, 76
Supervisors 3, 9, 12, 13, 14, 16, 17, 26, 27, 29, 30, 31, 35, 36, 38, 39, 40, 42, 44, 46, 60, 68, 70, 81, 89, 110, 112, 113, 114, 116, 117, 118, 119, 128

Take-home pay 40, 43, 49, 55, 57, 169
Technology 1, 2, 3, 4, 6, 7, 8, 9, 12, 13, 15, 24, 31, 46, 48, 49, 76, 80, 81, 89, 90, 119, 128, 130, 180
Telangana 171
Test of Association 83, 85, 87
Time-scale of pay 42, 138, 155, 159
Tool Manufacturing Plant 27-8
Trade union, see Unionism
Training, see Workers' training

Unemployment 11, 13, 44-5, 58, 59, 61, 62, 70, 133, 134, 138, 144, 173, 174, 182

Union force 9
Unionism 17, 136-7
Unionization 3
Uttar Pradesh 171

Vaishyas 38, 167

Wage-cutting 135
Wages 3, 4, 5, 6, 9, 10, 12, 13, 17, 26, 27, 28, 29, 30, 31, 42, 43, 44, 48, 77, 91, 110, 111, 112, 113, 114, 115, 116, 117, 118, 119, 128, 129, 130, 132, 133, 135, 136, 138, 154, 155, 156, 157, 158-9, 160, 163, 170, 171, 177, 178, 180, 182
Wagon Repair Workshop 23, 27
Welfare services 12, 64, 70, 155, 180
White-collar occupations 47, 174, 175, 179, 181, 182
Women workers 155, 158
Work, Image of 110-27
Work experience, *see* Employment experience
Work group 2, 4, 6, 8, 10, 13, 77, 110, 112, 113, 114, 115, 116, 117, 118, 129, 132, 156, 161
Work measurement 155, 157
Work performance 26, 158, 163
Work rhythms 5
Work rules 3, 4, 6, 9
Work simplification 4
Work standards 3, 4

Worker's earnings 5, 10, 51, 49, 63, 108, 119, 135, 138, 169-70, 174, 182, 183
Workers' education 5, 8, 11, 12, 61, 66, 67-9, 70, 82, 84-5, 89, 90, 119, 130, 131, 134, 176, 178-9, 181, 182
Workers' expectations 110, 111-3, 115, 116, 117, 120, 126, 133, 135
Workers' income 39-41, 43, 82, 83-4, 89, 90, 108, 130
Workers' perceptions 60, 61-3, 70, 110, 113-4, 115, 116, 122, 126, 131, 132, 175-80, 182, 183
Workers' reactions 110, 114-5, 116, 124, 126
Workers' training 5, 8, 11, 12, 26, 27, 28, 47-9, 61, 62, 63, 66, 67-9, 70, 132, 133, 134, 135, 138, 176, 178-9, 182, 183
Workforce 4, 11, 12, 17, 22, 28, 29, 30, 31, 35, 60, 61, 64, 67, 70, 71, 131, 132, 134, 137, 151, 152, 160, 182
  Social characteristics 34-59, 163-75
Working conditions 3, 5, 10, 12, 13, 26, 30, 77, 110, 112, 114, 115, 117, 118, 129, 132, 135, 136, 155, 158, 170, 180, 183
Workload 10, 26
Works committee 27